Legal Aliens

Legal Aliens

Gil Berkovich

iUniverse, Inc.
New York Bloomington Shanghai

Legal Aliens

iUniverse books may be ordered through booksellers or by contacting:

iUniverse
1663 Liberty Drive
Bloomington, IN 47403
www.iuniverse.com
1-800-Authors (1-800-288-4677)

ISBN: 978-0-595-51484-7 (pbk)
ISBN: 978-0-595-61917-7 (ebk)

Printed in the United States of America

Contents

Acknowledgments

I would like to thank my family for providing me with the stories and experiences I have written about, especially Sarah, Aaron and Barbara, who encouraged me to write, and Victor who was kind enough to read my rough draft.

Preface

I'm not famous, or even semi-famous for that matter. I wouldn't pay to read the life story of an unknown person, and I do not expect anyone else to. So why on earth would I write a memoir only a few people may want to read?

This is an attempt at preserving the stories and history of a very diverse set of colorful characters who contributed their DNA to make me. This was not intended to be a commercial venture.

I always wanted to know where I came from, who my ancestors were, what they were like, and what they did. I'm interested in knowing how they survived their particular set of circumstances. Our real life dramas, comedies, tragedies, and sex stories are anything but boring, and therefore worth recording.

Like most lives, ours are untidy and uneven, but still there is a certain balance to it. What seems disconnected is often not. Our world appears to work in circles. It's like the seasons which change, yet always come back to where they began.

The relatives in this memoir lived through the turbulent times of the twentieth and early twenty-first centuries and were shaped, as we all are, by the events around them. A hundred years from now, my relatives may wish to know what kind of gene pool they are swimming in. This is the un-chlorinated version of the wonderful, unpredictable, bizarre and eccentric people who make up our family.

1. Sleepless Nights

I often wake up in the middle of the night screaming. The slightest noise or movement sets me off. My wife finds this especially annoying as she starts screaming with me, not knowing what I am screaming about.

My kids fight with each other over the task of who gets to wake dad up. They know they will probably startle me, making me jump two feet off the bed, and then I would stand ramrod straight with my eyes closed, screaming at the top of my lungs as if someone were trying to kill me.

"Dad is nuts," they say as they run for cover.

"We didn't marry him, you did. It's your job to wake him, not ours," they would yell at their mom, as they scurried away promising never to wake me again.

The origin of this neurosis appears to be my *emmah*, the Hebrew word for mother. But, really, all she was doing was following doctor's orders, or at least the orders the way she understood them.

When she was pregnant with me, we lived in Israel, in a small town outside of Tel Aviv called Petach Tikvah. She was in her last trimester of her pregnancy, and contracted an illness from my older sister.

"Mrs. Berkovich," the doctor said, "you have rubella, also known as German measles. This is usually a mild childhood illness and is caused by a virus, but if the mother contracts the illness during pregnancy the illness poses a serious threat to the fetus."

As my mother sat in his office stunned, the doctor continued, "There is a good chance the child will be born with one or more birth defects. These abnormalities include eye defects, which result in blindness, hearing loss, mental retardation and less frequently, cerebral palsy. Some infected babies appear normal at birth and even during infancy, but the loss in hearing and eyesight can appear later."

Needless to say this caused my mother to go off the deep end, and in her case she didn't need to go far to get there. Thousands of babies were born with birth defects attributed to congenital rubella syndrome during an outbreak of rubella from 1962 through 1965. I was born in 1962.

My emmah was, and still is, a very spiritual person. She believes in all kinds of spirits ... good spirits, evil spirits, mischievous spirits, and even Voodoo spirits.

When a black cat happens to cross her path, she spontaneously begins to spit on the floor three times with a rapid "TU-TU-TU" to ward off the evil spirits. She wears a Hamsa, a five fingered hand amulet or pendant around her neck to protect against the *ayin raah* or the evil eye. The Hamsa hand is a symbol of both blessing and protection in Judaism.

Mom reads palms like a Gypsy and flips cups of Turkish coffee upside down to determine what the future holds by interpreting the images left by the coffee grounds. Astrology is an exact science to her; she takes it very seriously, and she was using it and every other magic trick she could think of to determine my outcome.

Obviously, the faith she was raised with, Judaism, also entered the equation, but, even with Judaism, she leans toward the mystical side of things with her belief in Kabalah. This offshoot of Judaism is at its core mysticism and numerology. Kabalists abandon ordinary meanings of words in the bible and give numerical values to letters and attribute mystical properties to both letters and numbers.

Due to the predicament Emmah was in, being pregnant with me and possibly giving birth to a baby with birth defects, she relied on her superstitions and mystical beliefs to get through this ordeal. After dozens of the Turkish coffees, hours of reading astrological charts and searching for secret messages in the Bible, her conclusion was I would turn out just fine, although, given what the doctor told my mother, she still felt she would need to test me constantly throughout my infancy to make certain I was not starting to lose my eyesight or hearing. In my opinion, this is the root cause of my waking up screaming at the slightest sound as an adult.

My mother decided in order to determine if I was going deaf as an infant, that she would take a large stainless steel pot from the kitchen along with a large metal spoon and sneak up by the side of my crib while I was sleeping and bang on the pot as loud as she could. It was like she was the lead percussionist banging on a snare drum in a marching band, but she was only few inches away from my head. This would obviously startle me, making me jump and scream at the top of my small lungs. Other times she would just quietly stalk my crib like a hunter and then all of a sudden jump up and scream "BOO" in my ear.

As bizarre as it seems, this was a great comfort to Emmah, who now knew, at least for that day, I was not deaf. She felt she had to continue this regimen until I was out of my infancy. While this made her sleep well, I, on the other hand, became a Pavlovian dog that still jumps and screams every time I hear any sound that awakens me.

Her other tests for eyesight were not as intrusive. At least I was already awake for those tests. The eyesight test consisted of following a finger or toy being moved from side to side while my eyes followed the object. As an adult I still get distracted easily, and I often find myself needing to watch objects moving from side to side.

My emmah's magic must have worked; other than being near-sighted, I can see, hear, smell, taste, and feel just fine.

2. Emmah

The environment leading up to my mother's birth was tumultuous. The world was beginning to unravel. In November of 1938, anti-Jewish riots were in full swing in Europe, shops were looted in Germany and Austria in what was called "Kristallnacht." The Nazi Party ruled Germany, and Hitler was its leader.

A core Nazi ideology was based on Hitler's obsession with achieving an Aryan master race. Racially pure people, according to the Nazi's, were non-Jewish Caucasians of Nordic stock. The Aryan look required blue eyes and blond or light colored hair and a stocky physique. Jews who were fortunate enough to have these physical characteristics were in less danger than those who had the physical characteristics of Jews portrayed in German propaganda films and newspapers. Those Jews had dark hair, dark eyes, big noses and a small stature. They were more likely to be captured and sent to concentration camps and never be seen again.

Hitler achieved the exact opposite of his purification objectives. In a sick Darwinian sense of survival of the fittest, more Jews today have blue eyes and blond hair than there may have been had the Holocaust not occurred. Jews who did not have these Aryan physical characteristics and who did not escape his murder machine were killed off, and that left the world with a disproportionate number of Aryan-looking Jews.

Few places on this planet were safe, especially for Jews. It was during those years, in what was then still British Palestine, Abraham Kalir, my grandfather, met Ahuva Chason, my grandmother. If it were not for World War II, the people who make up my family would never have come into contact with one another. That nightmare brought together humans from all corners of the globe and created a new fate for these people which would not have occurred otherwise.

Abraham Kalir was born in Kovnah, a city in Lithuania on the Baltic Sea. Yiddish or Jewish was a medieval language derived from a combination of German and Hebrew, and was written in the Hebrew alphabet, and was the language of choice in the city he was from. The Kalir family was lucky to have fled before the Germans and later the Russians occupied Lithuania. The Kalirs were Ashkenazi Jews. These Jews originated in Europe or Russia. Israel's founders were all Ashkenazi Jews. Most escaped either Hitler or the pogroms to come to Israel. The Chasons were Sephardic Jews. Sephardics originated in Spain, but due to the Spanish Inquisition around 1492 they fled or were expelled to Middle Eastern countries and eventually immigrated to Palestine from those countries.

Many Ashkenazi Jews considered themselves superior to Sephardic Jews in the 1930's and early 1940's. Sephardic Jews who had dark skin, hair, and eye color were treated as second-class citizens. They were generally less educated and poorer than their Ashkenazi brethren. These people had many limitations placed on them by the Arab countries they lived in, especially as far as academics and employment was concerned. Sephardic Jews held most of the menial jobs in Palestine at the time. They did the cleaning, cooking and hard manual labor. Few Sephardic Jews would ever get to marry an Ashkenazi Jew.

Ahuva's family consisted of her mother, Jamila, her two brothers's Avramino and Haim, and her younger sister Sima. Jamila, my great-grandmother, was only fourteen when she married Shabtai Chason and had her first son, Avramino, only nine months later.

Jamila's family was originally from Turkey. The family went to Alexandria, Egypt hoping they could improve their lot in life.

Shabtai Chason owned a shop in the market or souk in Alexandria, Egypt. The Souk was a maze of streets, narrow alleys and cobblestone thoroughfares. It was a noisy marketplace made up of artisans who sold goods from various Eastern countries like Morocco, Persia, Iraq, Lebanon, and Tunisia. It had stalls filled with soaps, jewelry, spices, brass grinders and coffee pots, textiles and rugs. The artisan's handcrafted goods were made of pottery, metal wood, glass and wool. Shabtai sold hand-woven rugs made of natural sheep's wool.

This ancient craft appeared as far back as the Old Testament. The nomads and peasants who made these rugs used a simple loom made of sticks oriented parallel to each other. These were mounted on the ground by pegs on which the strings of wool were tensed and then woven together. These simple devices were easily transferred from place to place allowing for the nomadic life that these sheepherders and artisans required. Every single knot was fastened separately by the women of these Arab tribes. Since each knot was tied separately they had the opportunity to add individual color and limitless patterns to their works of art. Their small hands would typically weave seven to ten thousand knots a day. It often took several years to complete a single rug. These hand woven threads were highly coveted and were extremely expensive at the turn of the century. They were sold primarily to the elite in Egyptian society.

Jamila was in her late twenties; she was the mother of three young children and was pregnant with her fourth. It was an ordinary Monday like any other. It was so ordinary it was hard for her to believe or absorb what had happened. "How can one's life change so totally in an instant?" she would often ask herself. Shabtai woke up and went to work. He had completed the sale of a large carpet when the Arabs who were observing him entered his shop. They robbed him of the money they saw him collect. When they asked for the money he gave it to them, but it wasn't enough. They stabbed him so many times in the chest his heart could no longer pump blood through his severed veins. Although death was always a part of life this end was both abrupt and premature.

Mrs. Jamila Chason was a young Jewish woman in an Arab country, a country without property, inheritance, civil or human rights as far as women were concerned. The rages of her emotions were seething within her. The agony, anger, bewilderment, despair, fear and guilt she felt would need to wait until she was able to get her family to safety. She barely had enough time to grieve for Shabtai. She knew for the sake of her family she needed to leave Egypt and head for the Promised Land as soon as possible.

In the early 1900's, Egyptian women would literally wear their wealth. My great grandmother wore gold bracelets from her wrists all the way up to her armpits. In order to leave this Middle Eastern country she sold most of her gold. She was a twenty-eight year old widow who would never marry again. Jamila was late in her third trimester of pregnancy with three toddlers when she arrived in British Palestine. They had no identity papers such as birth certificates or passports when they arrived, but luckily the administrators had not yet closed off the borders to Jews. The bureaucrats who oversaw the borders labeled anyone who came from a Middle Eastern country a Mizrahi, the Hebrew word for Easterners. Since Jamila did not have any documentation to prove who she was, they gave her the new Sur name Mizrahi on the documentation they provided her. This was meant as an insult. It was a scarlet letter of shame to signify to everyone that these were clearly Sephardic Jews.

As soon as Jamila gave birth to her fourth child and was told it was a girl she asked the nurses to take her away. She had prayed for a boy and wanted to at least honor her husband's memory by naming her son Shabtai. Jewish tradition does not allow one to be named for a living person, but it was a means to show respect for the dead by naming a baby after the person who passed away. My great grandmother was trying to alleviate some of her feelings of guilt. Jamila kept searching the time before Shabtai's death for evidence of her failure to help. She accused herself of negligence for not being there with him and not getting him the medical help that may have saved his life. This was pure nonsense; she was a mother with three children and pregnant with her fourth. Women were not allowed to interact with men who were not part of their family in Arab society. She could not work with her husband, but it did not stop her from accusing herself.

The nurses in the hospital named the girl Sima, short for Simcha, the female form of the Hebrew word for happiness. Jamila left the hospital without Sima and the baby was placed in an orphanage. She was alone in a foreign country with no means to support her children. This young widow pleaded for help from everyone she came in contact with. After a short while, she had no choice but to place her other children, Avramino, Haim and Ahuva in the orphanage as well.

When Jamila was finally able to find work in the kitchen of the hospital she had given birth in, she saved every coin she earned. She worked long days in the hundred plus degree heat of the kitchen. This facility didn't have any kind of ventilation or air conditioning. Her clothes were often drenched in sweat after she completed her shift, but she never missed a day of work. After several months of working in this dismal environment she went to the orphanage and took her four children home. It was her children that gave her the motivation and strength to get out of bed each day.

For Ahuva, Sima, Avramino and Haim the immediate decline in their quality of life caused immeasurable harm. Young kids are ego-centric. They often feel and believe their conduct causes everything around them. Some children feel their parent died because of something they did or didn't do. They were angry their father died, and they never got over the feeling of abandonment. The loss of attention caused by Jamila's need to work and Shabtai's death led them to make decisions they may have not otherwise made.

When Ahuva met Abraham she was in her late teens. Abraham was a tall, fair-skinned man with deep blue eyes and light brown hair. My grandfather was a flattering and seductive person. He was good-looking and he took full advantage of it. Abraham could make you feel as though his world was very special, and if he let you into it, you too would be special. When a total stranger, who is attractive, makes a young naïve girl feel special, she becomes easy prey for a predator and narcissist like Abraham, and Ahuva was very young and very naïve.

Ahuva got pregnant by Abraham. The only person she told was Haim, her younger brother. Their mother, Jamila, did not know about Ahuva's condition. Ahuva and Haim knew that if she found out the shame would kill her. Haim did the only thing he could; he confronted Abraham and told him if he did not marry his sister he would have no choice but to kill him. Both Arabs and Jews practiced honor killings then. Abraham took Haim's threat seriously and married Ahuva before my mother's birth.

Jaffa Kalir, my emmah, was born in 1940 in Palestine, shortly after Abraham and Ahuva's marriage. (My mother was a Sabra, which was a metaphor for those people who were born in Israel. A Sabra is a fruit with a prickly outside and a sweet interior.) Emmah came from what Jews at the time would call a mixed marriage. There was a huge cultural divide between the European Ashkenazi Jews and the Middle Eastern Sephardic Jews. Sephardic Jews were called Arab Jews. They shared the same religion as Ashkenazi Jews, but they were culturally Arab, not European. These Middle Eastern Jews were often poor and uneducated, unlike many of the Ashkenazis. The Kalirs came from a long line of rabbis and scholars. The

Chasons sold carpets in the souk in Egypt. The respective families did not approve of each other, and obviously Abraham had never really intended to marry Ahuva. Soon after Ahuva and Abraham were married, they were also divorced. Divorce in 1940 was scandalous, but it was the lesser of two evils. An unwed mother would have been ostracized and my mother would have been considered illegitimate. So being a child from a broken, mixed marriage family, as bad as that may be was the best outcome mom could have expected.

My mother's parents may explain some of her eccentricities, but it was her life experience that accounted for her unique personality. Mom has the biggest heart of anyone I know. She cares deeply about people and especially her kids. When she isn't dealing with her own problems, she takes on other people's problems as if they were her own. But my mother lacks the capacity to manage her emotions; she has no self-control, no ability to have an inner dialogue with herself, everything she ever felt she also needed to express. Words come out of my mother's mouth without any filters. Sometimes expressing yourself could be a good thing, but having to express every feeling, more often than not, leads to trouble.

Emmah was not raised by, nor did she live with, her mother as a child. Her father's mother, Sarah Kalir, raised her. Even though she grew up with Abraham's mother, she would rarely, if ever, see him. In essence her only parent was this widowed elderly woman, who she called Bobbeh, the Yiddish word for grandmother. Bobbeh was a very petite Lithuanian woman who was also very kind and giving. The problem for Emmah was that Bobbeh had nothing but love and faith to give her. Bobbeh lived in a three-room shack in what is now a nice part of Herzliya, Israel. Her home was so small you could barely fit the table, chairs, and beds they had in it. In the 1940's this was in the middle of nowhere. The shack she lived in was hidden in a small orange grove. It had a tin roof and looked like it was put together with remnants of garbage and whatever other odd materials could be cobbled together. It was a roof over my mother's head, but not much more.

Food was another problem; they did not have enough to eat, and my mother would often get bread covered with bugs. Bobbeh told Emmah the food was still good and to just wipe them off. Until this day, my mother refuses to eat rye bread with seeds. The seeds remind her of the bugs she used to see crawling on her food, and she can't stand to look at it. I have, thank goodness, never known real hunger, but I can tell you it leaves real, permanent scars on one's psyche.

When you live in a hot climate like Israel under conditions approaching squalor, cleanliness becomes an absolute necessity to avoid serious illness. Today cleanliness is an obsession with my mother. She loves disinfectants and uses Pine Sol by the gallon; she bleaches the kitchen countertops and uses small toothbrushes to clean every corner of her home. To say you could eat off my mother's floor is an understatement. I think her home would meet all of the clinical standards of a surgical unit in a hospital.

Emmah did learn a lot from her grandmother during her childhood. Bobbeh spoke fluent Yiddish and mom obviously learned the language while she was growing up. The thing is, only Askenazi Jews speak Yiddish. So the fact Emmah spoke Yiddish made people think she was Askenazi, and it helped her mask the fact she came from a mixed marriage.

Faith was an integral part of my mother's upbringing. Bobbeh was an Orthodox Jewish woman and raised my mom in that small tin shack to be Orthodox. My mother was taught the entire mitzvahs, Jewish commandments, and was told to adhere to them. There are 613 Jewish mitzvahs, which is a lot of rules for any kid to adhere to. Keeping the Sabbath holy was a big one, it is number four on the top ten lists of commandments that Moses brought down from Mount Sinai, and my mother was told she had better adhere to it. Back then if the religious authorities couldn't inspire you to avoid sinning, they would scare the hell out of you instead. On Sabbath you were not supposed to work, harvest, create or destroy anything. Sabbath was the day of rest. During the time of the ancient Jewish Sages, the penalty for not keeping the Sabbath holy was death.

When Emmah was twelve, sometime after her Bat Mitzvah, or the age a young women is considered to be an adult by Jewish law, she was walking home from a friend's house and forgot it was Sabbath and picked a flower. Mom was certain that G-d would shortly strike her down. She went into her small room in the shack she lived in with her grandmother and waited for the lightning bolt. Finally Bobbeh came in to the room and in a concerned tone asked, "What's wrong?"

Emmah shut her eyes tight, but the tears ran down anyway. She said in a low quivering voice, "I will be dead shortly. I broke the rules of Sabbath and picked a flower on my way home today."

Bobbeh replied in a soft, light-hearted manner, "G-d does not strike down those who inadvertently break his rules, and he always allows you to repent if you make a mistake. Don't worry," she said, "G-d will not strike you down."

After this discussion two things happened. Firstly, my mother began to have some skepticism about Judaism and became more mystical, and secondly, she still feels G-d will strike her down in the near future and expects she will be dead at any moment. I don't think I have had a conversation with my mother in the last twenty years in which she does not tell me she will surely soon be dead, and I should be nice to her, or I will forever regret it.

3. Abbah

I'm really not sure what name to call my father or *abbah* in Hebrew. My father's name is Hiam, Tzvi, Herman, Hiam-Tzvi or Harry. It all depends on which legal document you're looking at. He isn't quite sure which name was really given to him at birth, but these days he goes by Tzvi in Hebrew and Harry in English.

His date of birth is also a mystery, he has two, and it was either September 4th or 6[th.] When my father looked through my grandfather's prayer book or Siddur, he saw that my grandfather had noted the birth of all of his children on the back cover. It noted my father's birth date as the 4th of September. Since my father was born at home, and not in a hospital, they waited two days to make certain he would survive before they informed the authorities of his birth. All of his legal documents therefore recorded his birth date as September 6[th.]

In 1935 Meir, Alte, Abbah and his two sisters Esther and Zipora arrived in British Palestine as refugees from Czechoslovakia. Abbah was just two years old. It was only a few weeks earlier that my grandfather's maid came running and screaming into his house to tell him they had killed his animals. When my grandfather went into his barn to see what she was talking about, he discovered that all of his horses had their legs cut off. Anti-Semitic threats were common in the small village of Repine where they lived, but this time he felt physical harm might come to him or his family if he stayed there. Meir was a very visible man in this small town; he owned the local market, the flourmill, the lumberyard and most of the land in the surrounding area. He leased the land to local farmers, who were not Jewish, for a percentage of the profits they generated from their crops. He had a large home and lots of servants. It's typical for people to resent the wealthiest man in town, and Meir was that man. He was an easy target for the Anti-Semitism growing at this time throughout Europe.

Luckily for him, several young Zionists from Palestine had visited him to see if they could convince him to move to what they hoped would one day be their own country. Zionism was the national movement for the return of the Jewish people to their homeland, and the resumption of Jewish sovereignty in the Land of Israel. For centuries, Jews had to survive in alien lands and among alien cultures, and now they had a chance to have their own country. They told him how valuable he would be in the founding of this country and how much they needed experts in agriculture and business to help build the infrastructure needed for what was then a neglected backwater.

Meir decided to go on a trip to Palestine with his family to see what it was like, just in case conditions in his homeland deteriorated. Every report he received from his family confirmed it was deteriorating. They sent him money, but other than those limited funds, and the suitcases he had with him, he basically had to start his life over. Finally his former country was handed over to Hitler, and Germany fully occupied it.

He never returned to Czechoslovakia. Those people foolish enough to try to get back to Eastern Europe in order to get their possessions ended up in concentration camps, a fate my grandfather and his immediate family luckily avoided. But my grandfather came close to making that mistake. After living over a year in Palestine with his money running out, Meir became desperate. He asked a friend to lend him money to go back home to sell some of his possessions, but his friend did not have enough to lend my grandfather, so my grandfather stayed in Palestine. The friend who went back to Czechoslovakia was never seen again.

Grandfather's faith and the Jewish traditions he was raised with, were a central part of who he was. Meir was a serious man who loved business. While other people talk about the weather, food, politics, or social issues my grandfather would want to know what you did for a living, what you produced, how was it manufactured, and what the profit margins were. Meir and I would often talk about finances. When I asked him how he made his money in Czechoslovakia, he declared confidently, "I always bought high and sold low."

I couldn't help but blurt out, "Grandfather, I went to business school, and what you are saying is the exact opposite of what they taught us in school."

He replied flatly, "Well, I never went to business school, but if you follow what the Talmud says chances are you too will succeed." The Talmud is a collection of ancient rabbinic writings, and is the basis of much of the authority in Judaism. The instructions he gave me were to "Study the market, and when you were in a depressed market, you pay a little more than your competitor for the property or business you were trying to buy. Word then usually spread you were paying more than your competitors and you get to buy more and see more deals than your competitors. When the market is strong and business is great and you are selling your property or business, you sell for just a little less than you competitors do. You get your deal done while the others languish on the market."

The other piece of advice I received was what I call the divine diversification strategy. My grandfather said, "according to the Talmud, you were supposed to divide your assets into three categories. A third of your net worth was supposed to be in real estate, one third in your business and or inventory, and one third in liquid assets such as cash." Meir may have not had the formal education I had, but he was very astute when it came to business.

My grandmother, or Safta in Hebrew, was a true homemaker; she would cook all-day and made certain that you also ate all day. She would often give my mother a hard time about how skinny I looked. She made my mother feel like it was her fault I was thin and she wasn't feeding me enough. When we would visit my grandparents, Alte would bring sandwiches to the airport just in case we were starving and couldn't possibly make it all the way to her home, which was only twenty minutes away.

Meir met his wife Shosi on their wedding day. It was an arranged marriage. Their parent's made what was called a *schiduch* or a match, before they ever laid eyes on each other. Earlier, I referred to my grandmother as Alte, but on their wedding day, Meir married Shosi. When a Jewish person becomes seriously ill, he will often take a new name, just in case the angel of death comes looking for him. The angel of death is supposed to get confused and not know whom to take, so hopefully he doesn't take anyone. My grandmother changed her name to Alte after an illness later in her life, and never used the name Shosi again.

Like most marriages of the time, a bride came with a dowry. The wealthier the groom, the larger the dowry had to be, and my grandfather was a wealthy man. So my great-grandfather whose name was Isaac Jakobovich decided to pay my grandfather with promissory notes for his daughter's dowry. He signed the notes and gave them to my grandfather, but he never paid a dime on them. This was a source of great shame for my grandfather, who obviously would never let any outsider know he was swindled. On the contrary, he would tell others what a huge dowry he got because he was such a catch. Each and every time I visited my grandfather in Israel, he would pull out all of these notes and he would describe in detail how my great-grandfather stiffed him. He would then jokingly threaten to send my grandmother back to where she came from. I finally asked my grandfather for one of these notes. It still hangs on my office wall.

Abbah was Meir and Alte's only son. He was the Prince of his household. Safta doted on dad; she had inexhaustible sympathy for him, and for that matter, all of her children. If my dad ever misbehaved, my grandmother would hit herself and pull her own hair out, but Dad never ever had a hand laid on him in anger. The logic was he would feel guilty about what he was doing and stop doing it. I'm not sure it worked, though, because when I saw my grandmother later in life, she didn't seem to have much hair left in her head, and I don't think my Abbah ever felt guilty about it.

Safta was a short woman, and by the time she was a grandmother she was very overweight. Alte had these big jowls which would shake when she laughed, which was often. She had deep blue eyes and a perpetual smile on her face. You could tell instantly anytime you saw her how genuinely happy she was to see you. She would always welcome you with a great big hug and a kiss on the cheek.

Alte and Meir would often sit out on the front porch of their Petach Tikvah home on an old, tattered, dilapidated, sagging sofa they left outdoors. My grandmother would sit with her hands clasped twirling her thumbs forward and backward over and over again, like a Ferris wheel going forward and then backward, while my grandfather would be in front of a fan in his white undershirt trying to stay cool. They both waited with anticipation for their kids to come home. My Abbah always knew he had parents who adored him.

Dad barely completed what would today be considered a high school education, and at the age of sixteen and a half he was drafted into the Israeli Army. After his basic training he became a tank instructor and maintenance officer. Tank warfare consisted of two primary objectives; you shoot the other guy first and you get the heck out of the area after you do. The faster one can make the tank move and the farther the artillery can reach, the bigger the advantage one has over their enemy. Israel received numerous used Sherman tanks from World War II from the Americans. What Israel was especially good at was adapting other's technology to the specific needs it had. My father modified the American Sherman tanks by replacing their engines with larger round nine cylinder aircraft engines. This made them faster than any other tank at the time. They also modified the Sherman's cannon to substantially increase the range of their artillery. But these modifications also caused a lot of problems. The engine was round and they needed to continuously rotate it because the oil would leak into the plugs and made it difficult to start the engine. In addition the clutch stuck a lot, and each time the clutch stuck, they needed to remove what was a huge and bulky engine to replace it. These tradeoffs were still worth the lives saved by having faster tanks with a more distant firing range. Although Israel was in a technical state of war with its neighbors from the day it declared independence in 1948, my father did not have to actively fight in a war in the two years three months he served in the army.

Today, women are the primary tank instructors for the Israeli Army. They teach the men how to drive, maintain and fire these weapons. Israel is one of the few countries in the world that drafts women into the army. Since the country's inception on May 14, 1948, women have been an integral part of the security of Israel.

Abbah was discharged from the army when he was nineteen. He later had various jobs driving trucks and buses and also owning and operating an automobile repair shop.

My Abbah was twenty-three and my Emmah was just sixteen when they met. My mother had long, black, wavy hair brushed back from her Egyptian forehead, green eyes, and olive-colored skin like her mother's. According to my father, the first time he laid eyes on my mother, he pointed her out to his friend and said, "She will one day be my wife."

I don't believe in love at first sight, and I think anyone who acts on his first impressions without knowing what he is are getting into is foolhardy. Neither one of my parents had any idea what was in store for them. I still find it incredible to think how young and inexperienced we are when we make one of the most important decisions of our lives. Sometimes I think the tradition of arranged marriages makes more sense. My grandparents lived their entire lives together, and the divorce rate amongst this older generation was almost nonexistent.

My grandparent's were not thrilled at the idea of Tzvi marrying Jaffa. They knew very little about her, and she looked Sephardic, but then again she could speak Yiddish, so how bad could she be.

I cannot even begin to imagine how anyone could be ready for marriage at sixteen. For my Emmah, marriage was an escape from extreme poverty, living with an elderly grandmother and the distant parents she hardly knew. She was not ready for marriage, children, or anything else life had in store for her, but back then all you could hope for was that the next thing would be better than what you had at the time.

4. A "Happy" Social Hall

Hiam, Tzvi, Herman Berkovich was married to Jaffa Kalir in a social hall named "Happy" in Petach Tikvah, Israel in 1957. In Hebrew the word for happy is pronounced Gil. My parents had such a good time at their wedding reception that they decided to name me after a social hall. "Hi, I'm Happy Berkovich." Obviously, I couldn't go through life with a name like Happy. So I decided to keep the Hebrew transliteration of the word Gil in English. I just tell everyone that Gil is short for Gil-Bert. Gilbert works in a lot of languages English, Spanish, and even French, but Happy just doesn't cut it in any language. I don't know why my parents just couldn't name my older sister Gila, the female form of the Hebrew word for Happy. She was born first, four years earlier than I was. Their reception had occurred only one year prior to her birth, and it was fresh in their minds. But no, they decided to wait until I was born to name me "Happy" because they liked the social hall they had their wedding in. I have to look at the bright side, it could have been far worse for me; they could have gotten married in a social hall named *Sameach*, another form of the word happy. Just think about going through life with a name like that.

Given the fact that my father has three to four first names, one would think they could have at least given me a middle name. But it's not the tradition in Israel. So I have no middle name. People think I am lying when I tell them I have no middle name. They keep asking me what it is, as if I'm ashamed of whatever it is. So I make up a middle name just to appease them. This week my middle name is Bert. I also get the free mailing labels from charities that refuse to believe that I do not have a middle name. My mailing labels are all printed G.I. Berkovich.

My name had the potential to make me a very unhappy person, if it weren't for one thing; my older sister got the name Vered. Vered in Hebrew means Rose, but the transliteration of Vered in English does not work. She didn't like the name Rose in English; she thought it reminded her of an old lady, so she kept her Hebrew name. But with a name like Vered, Americans just don't get it. They call her Vera, Voorah, Velvet, you name it, but Vered is not a name they expect anyone to have. Knowing she has it far worse than I do, as far as her name goes, does make me "Happy."

5. John

Sima, grandmother's younger sister, had met and married an English soldier in Palestine while it was still under British mandate. He was a Christian. Bending tradition was one thing, but marrying a non-Jew was the breaking point for Jamila. My great grandmother vowed to never speak to or recognize the existence of her daughter again. She sat Shiva for Sima. Sitting Shiva is an ancient Jewish tradition that mourners perform. For seven days the mourner does not leave their home and they do not sit upon chairs of normal height. The custom is to be seated on the floor or the earth itself. It is a physical adjustment to one's emotional state. It is a lowering of the body to the level of one's feelings. It is a reminder of the very earth the relative has been interred to. Shiva is referred to as the "Days of Bitterness." Someone who publicly and purposefully disowns their Jewish faith, practices, laws and traditions is mourned as dead.

Jews do not accept the ancient pagan custom of tearing the flesh and hair, which would symbolize the loss of one's own flesh and blood. Instead the expression of grief is the rending or tearing of garments. This tearing is a psychological relief, it allows the mourner to vent his pent-up anguish by an act of destruction. In addition to wearing a torn garment and sitting on the floor or a low stool, the mourner wears slippers, as leather shoes are forbidden, and refrains from grooming or shaving, and all of the mirrors in the home are covered in a dark fabric so that the mourner does not see himself during this anguished period.

When the British Mandate ended in May 1948, both Sima and her husband were no longer welcome in what was now Israel, and shortly thereafter they moved to England. Seven sad years had passed since Jamila had spoken to or seen her daughter Sima. Ahuva, her eldest daughter, had been pleading with her mother to forgive and recognize Sima again. After Jamila fasted for forty-eight hours and pleaded with G-d to allow her to break her vow to him she finally gave Ahuva permission to travel to England to make peace with her youngest daughter.

When Ahuva finally traveled to England to visit her sister, she met John Shulver who was a neighbor of Sima's and her husbands. John was already in awe of Sima; she was the most independent, smart, and exotic women he had ever encountered. But she was already married, so when he met Ahuva, he assumed she must be a lot like her sister.

I have come to the conclusion G-d makes certain that siblings are never alike. My great-grandmother used to say, "Kids are like your hands. You have ten fingers and no two fingers are exactly alike. Some are larger, some are fatter, and they are all different. But if you cut off any two of your different fingers, the pain from the loss will be the same for both fingers."Although Ahuva was beautiful and exotic she had no other similarities with her sister Sima, but she was about to cause the same pain to her mother as her sister had. Ahuva got married for the second time to John Shulver, a Christian. She had gone to England to heal the rift in her family caused by her sister's break with Jewish tradition, and then she decided to marry a non-Jew herself.

John, on the other hand, had been dating an Englishwoman, but she wanted her mother to live with them if they got married, and the last thing John wanted was having his future mother-in-law living with him. So John left this girl for Ahuva. What he didn't know at the time was that he was trading an English mother-in-law for an Egyptian mother-in-law named Jamila.

It seems my grandmother had a thing for marrying men she could not speak to. She could not speak Yiddish, Russian or English, and her husbands spoke neither Arabic nor Hebrew. I don't know how many times I've heard how important it is to communicate with your spouse in order for the marriage to work. We are told husbands need to learn to listen better. What my grandmother's experience taught me was when your wife tells you her problems, you don't have to solve them, just act like you're listening. Ahuva's husbands listened to her just fine, but it was the fact they never understood a word she was saying that often helped them avoid conflict.

John and Ahuva settled in England and had a baby girl named Carmela. She lived only three short months. John and Ahuva never spoke about Carmela. It was only in the process of researching our family history I was told that I had another aunt at one time. Child mortality rates back then were much higher than they are today. England was cold, wet, and gray, and after the loss of their child Ahuva talked John into moving to Israel to start over.

John agreed to convert to Judaism once they immigrated to Israel. This was most likely in order to appease Jamila. Jews do not proselytize; they do not go out and try to convert anyone to the faith. As a matter of fact, the Rabbis actively discourage Christians from converting to Judaism. They feel if they convert a non-Jew who then doesn't keep the commandments of the faith they are partially responsible for a sinner who would not have sinned otherwise. The rules of Judaism are for Jews; they are not required of non-Jews. The Rabbis try to make certain the person really wants to convert. They discourage the potential convert and make him or her come back numerous times pleading for the conversion. Then there is the extensive studying and testing required of the convert. But the biggest issue for an adult male convert to Judaism is the required circumcision. A circumcision is the act of removing or cutting back the foreskin of the penis. The Jewish rite of brit milah, "covenant of circumcision," is in the book of Genesis and translated in the Art Scroll Tanach as follows:

"This is my covenant, which you shall keep between Me and you and your descendents after you: Every male among you shall be circumcised. You shall circumcise the flesh of your foreskin, and that shall be the sign of the covenant between Me and you. At the age of eight days every male among you shall be circumcised, throughout your generations. Thus, My covenant shall be in your flesh for an everlasting covenant. An uncircumcised male who will not circumcise the flesh of his foreskin he should be cut off from my people; he has invalidated My covenant."

I can't imagine the pain associated with the procedure preformed on an adult male. When Jewish infants have this procedure performed, they are only eight days old. Only Abraham, our faith's patriarch, at the age of ninety-nine, and converts had this done as adults. John must have been crazy about my grandmother or just plain crazy.

6. *Vered and Edna*

My older sister Vered was born 1958 in a hospital in Petach Tikvah, Israel. What makes this unusual wasn't Vered's birth; it was Edna's birth. My grandmother Ahuva gave birth to Edna only three months earlier than my mother. My mother was six months pregnant when her mother gave birth to Edna. Edna is a half sister to my mother, and our Aunt Edna is only three months older than Vered. This for the first time brought my mother and her mother closer together. They now had something in common. They both had infant daughters to raise. Although they were aunt and niece, Edna and Vered would grow up as sisters.

It's ironic that while my mother was constantly testing my hearing as an infant to determine if I were going deaf, it was my sister, Vered, who lost her hearing. Vered ran a very high fever when she was an infant, and it caused the total loss of her hearing in her right ear. Since she could hear fine in her left ear, this was not detected early, so she never went through the pot and pan testing I went through. Today anytime my sister wants to tune you out all she needs to do is turn a deaf ear to you.

We have album books full of Vered and Edna's baby pictures. It was when I realized there weren't any baby pictures of me that I began searching for some answers. I doubt anyone has ever lived who did not at some point wonder, especially during adolescence, if he or she had been adopted. I grew up thinking the stork left me on the wrong doorstep or I was possibly switched in the hospital with another baby. Given the chaos in a typical Israeli hospital when I was born, it was a definite possibility.

My mother caught me looking through her papers in her closet.

"What are you doing?" she asked in a low and threatening voice.

I responded "I'm looking for the adoption papers."

"What adoption papers?" she inquired.

"My adoption papers" I said.

"What are you talking about?" she retorted in an annoyed tone.

I then explained that "I have never seen a single baby picture of me and you have tons of baby pictures of Vered. I am aware of the fact I don't look like anyone else in the family, and I'm assuming you never told me I'm adopted. I know you owned a camera, Vered's pictures prove it, and I wouldn't believe you if you told me you lost the camera after I was born."

She then said without any hesitation, "You were an ugly child; we thought you wouldn't appreciate having a lot of pictures of you to remind you how you looked when you were a baby." I was always told every mother thought their child was beautiful, but not my mother, she always said exactly what she thought.

My sister and I did not have the normal sibling rivalry that most brothers and sisters have. Even though she was only four years older, Vered had a very maternal instinct, and she looked out for me. My sister and I may have drawn from the same gene pool but we had very different childhoods. My parents' expectations of my sister and me were very different. As a male, I was expected to be the family breadwinner. Academic and later financial success was an expectation everyone had of me. My sister, on the other hand, was expected to be a wife and mother, so if she never achieved much in school it was not a major concern to my parents.

Edna was in essence an only child. Ahuva and John never had another child after Edna, probably for good reason. Some of the smartest, best-adjusted children in the world are only children.

They are typically more motivated in school, more likely to continue higher education and more driven to succeed. Edna was the opposite of a typical only child: she was not motivated in school, and she would never go on to college. Maybe Edna never acted like a typical single child because she really never lacked siblings. She did have a much older half sister, and Vered and I acted like surrogate siblings.

7. Going Down to America

Life was extremely harsh during the late 1950's and early 1960's. Israel had very limited infrastructure in terms of communication, transportation, or health care. My father decided he wanted to give his family a future he did not see for us in Israel. The conflict between the Arabs and Jews was always going to be a zero sum game. When you have a conflict over the same asset, in this case one small piece of land, there can't be two winners. One party will ultimately win and the other will lose. With this conflict my father realized the resolution would not come anytime soon or possibly even ever. I was only an infant at the time, but the thought of my having to grow up and become a soldier weighed heavily on my parents.

My father visited the United States in 1953 when he was single, and he liked what he saw. Dad wanted to go to a free country, which was not under the constant threat of war, and where opportunities were unlimited.... America.

When someone leaves Israel, the Israeli's refer to it as going "down" to whatever country you are going to, and when someone immigrates to Israel it is referred to as going "up" or making Aliyah or an ascension to the Holy Land. Jews who do not live in Israel live in what is called the Diaspora, a word from Greek meaning a scattering. The psychology of this is evident; the founders of Israel wanted Jews to move to the Promised Land and wanted to discourage them from leaving. A person was considered a fallen person when he left Israel. But Israel was a free country, and it did not prohibit people from leaving.

Meir and Alte also didn't want my father to leave and discouraged him from doing so by not offering much assistance if he did. But he was determined to go ahead and strike out on his own. It seems all of the men in the family have two primary personality traits, determination and stubbornness.

We were sailing into the unknown, on a long journey from which we may not come back. Mother spread all of their worldly possessions out and began to pack them. She was never sure of what she would need, on this trip or for that matter any trip we took, so she always packed everything.

In 1963, Tzvi, Jaffa, Vered and I boarded a ship of Greek registry from the port of Haifa and were bound for New York. I was only ten months old when this transatlantic journey began. I was told I was sick and crying the entire time. I had an ear infection and my father had to carry me in his arms for the duration of the trip. The stress of having a sick baby on a long journey to a new country must have been extremely difficult.

Although twelve million immigrants passed through Ellis Island in its heyday from 1892 through 1924, we were obviously not among them. Ellis Island closed its doors in 1954. Mass immigration at the turn of the century was not controlled really. There was no passport and no visa requirement. No papers were needed. You just bought a ticket, jumped on a boat and sailed to America and took your chance to get through Ellis Island. As long as you had no disease, or were not obviously sick, and were not about to try to overthrow the government, you could get through Ellis Island. In 1963 we needed all of the proper papers. We needed visas and passports to get into the United States, but luckily being sick was not as much of an issue, since I would probably have been sent back to Israel if I had had to go through Ellis Island at the turn of the century. We had come this country legally, but we were as alien as any immigrant who ever stepped foot on American soil. It was as if we had landed on another planet and had to learn to breathe new air. We had traveled far in terms of both place and time.

After our ship docked in Manhattan, and our papers were checked by customs, we were picked up by my one of my father's friends Isaac Duvduvani and taken to Brooklyn, one of the five boroughs of New York.

Emmah was in total shock at the magnitude of New York. But it wasn't the size of the buildings or the beauty of the sun's rays smacking into the mirrored facades of the massive skyscrapers that caught her attention. It was something else entirely. On the way to Isaac's home we drove past a cemetery and my mother noticed the tombstones. She asked Abbah "Why are the tombstones so close to one another?"

He answered, "Land prices in New York are very high, and in order to save money, New Yorkers bury their dead standing up."

Emmah shook her head from side to side, possibly not believing him, and then said, "Make certain my body is sent back to Israel if I die here. Make certain I am never buried in New York."

When we first got to Brooklyn, we lived in the basement of the home of Isaac and Rochelle Duvduvani. Unlike Manhattan, a center of commerce, Brooklyn had the promising life of residential neighborhoods and lower rents. Within a week or so my father found an apartment in a neighborhood called Borough Park. Borough Park is one of three neighborhoods in Brooklyn with significant Jewish populations and which consisted mainly of immigrants from both Israel and what is now the ex-Soviet Union. The local shops all had signs in Hebrew, Yiddish and Russian. The Hasidic shop owners had black hats set atop their yarmulke or skull cap, and the curls of hair, or Payyes, were visible at the sides of their heads. They also wore the same long black coats their ancestors did in Poland. The married women covered their hair with wigs as a sign of modesty; and nearly all of them were pushing baby carriages.

Brooklyn was as vast as its inhabitants and changed every few blocks, as did the shops, signs and the languages you heard. In New York, the Chinese had China Town, the Italians had Little Italy, and the Jews had Borough Park. What was especially great about New York was the ethnic stew of immigrants. You had Russians, Irish, Italian, Pakistanis and Chinese all living together. We would all compare our various diasporas and argue over whose historic pain was greater. The Jews often won these arguments, but the Irish would come in a close second. No one group was dominant. This was a fusion of ethnicity unlike anywhere else on the planet. Someone who could not speak the language, who came from a different country or culture, was not considered unique, it was the norm. The main thing one needed to learn was how to cuss in seven or eight languages. People somehow related to multicultural profanities. Not being able to speak the local language would be an insurmountable obstacle in any another country, but it was not an impediment to success in America.

Although my dad worked long hours, his work quickly paid off and he was starting to make a decent living. Dad initially found work in a gas station in Brooklyn owned by Italian immigrants. Only three months after learning the business in terms of how things worked in America versus how they had worked in Israel, my father purchased a gas station of his own. Gas stations in the 1960's were totally different from today's stations. Firstly, they all had repair shops with bays and lifts in them, not the mini-markets most stations have today. The pumps were not automated with an attendant sitting in a cozy interior space and not having to come out to your car. Back then you could not just swipe you credit card and pump your own gas. The attendant had to come out to your car in the rain, freezing cold, or summer heat and ask you what kind of gas you wanted, and how much you wanted and then he had to pump the gas for you. Cars were not full of computer chips to tell you what was wrong with the car if it was attached to a diagnostic computer; you had to figure it out yourself.

Ahuva, John and Edna moved to Brooklyn a few blocks away from where we were living sometime after we arrived. Edna, who was five years old at the time, was the only one who didn't want to go to America. She had seen the film "Birth of a Nation" by D.W. Griffith and was scared to go. The original title of Griffith's movie was "The Clansman," and it was an anti-black, pro-Ku Klux Klan, racist and vicious film. The Klan still uses the movie as a recruitment piece. It depicts the KKK as heroes and Southern blacks as villains. Edna protested, "Americans wear white hoods and bed sheets, burn crosses and kill black people. I don't want to go there." But she was told the movie was not true and that was not what America was like, so she eventually was convinced it was safe to go. John worked with my father at his gas station. He was a top-notch mechanic, and my father needed the help. Ahuva worked in the cafeteria at our school, and Edna was enrolled in the same school and attended the same classes as my sister, Vered.

Throughout this period of our lives our home would be a temporary way station for the immigrants who came to the United States. They would live on our sofas and in our basement until they found work and established themselves. Some times it lasted for months. These people were our relatives, or family friends, or friends of friends. Our home became a revolving door for people coming to America. But my family never forgot the help they received when they came to this country, and they made certain they would help others in the same way.

Conditions in Israel a few years after our arrival were still very difficult. The wars, the general state of the economy, and the overall quality of life were taking a toll on its people. Israelis who decided to leave Israel made a bargain with themselves and their families. Once they were established in another country, they promised to help support Israel and their families by sending funds. It was a way to justify moving to another country after centuries of fighting and finally attaining the goal of our own Jewish State.

8. Well Done

America has very useful ways of helping to maintain a civilized and orderly society. One would always see people patiently waiting in line. They actually read the signs displayed in public places and obeyed the rules. Service in Israel was non-existent. The concept of waiting in line or waiting to be seated was totally foreign to us. If you were foolish enough to wait your turn in Israel, people would think you are some sort of fool or sucker. There were no lines, no waiting, and no rules. It was a melee of pushing, shoving and cutting in front of the next guy. In the U.S. you do not seat yourself in a restaurant without permission, even if the place is empty. My family was not familiar with this custom. They ignored all signs like "Please Wait to Be Seated." If they saw an open table in a restaurant, it was their table. This practice annoyed the hostess and our waitress to no end, and that was even before they took an order from us. My parents could hardly speak English. The waitress would rattle off a list of salad dressings. "We have Italian, Creamy Italian, Garlic Italian, French, Ukrainian, Moldavian, Azerbaijani, Thousand Island, Ranch, and Blue Cheese etc ..." My mother and father obviously never heard of eleven different types of salad dressings. They weren't certain what salad dressings were. This sounded like a list of the members of the United Nations. The server would describe our food choices with incomprehensibly large words. We would sit quietly until the waitress finished listing all of the items on the menu, then we would ask her to repeat them again and again. I'm sure she thought we were all brainless nitwits. Most times our meal selections were entirely based on what looked good on other people's tables. My parents would act like they were heading to the restroom only to check out what everyone else in the restaurant had in front of them. If it looked good, they would point at the table and say, "We want that." When the poor server would finally arrive with our food, my mother would always send it right back to the kitchen telling them, "I like it WELL DONE." "My food has to be dead, very dead, not alive," she would tell the waitress. The waitress would then say, "Excuse me, but this animal is not only dead; it has been cremated." This process would often require the food to be sent back at least three times or until the waitress delivered what looked like charcoal. On several occasions the chef would come out of the kitchen to see who the nut was that kept sending the food back to him until he purposefully burnt it. He thought he was getting back at this nightmare of a customer. But burnt to a crisp was exactly how my mother liked her food.

9. Yeshiva

My sister was enrolled in a Yeshiva, a Jewish religious school called Ahi-Ezer on Ocean Parkway, a four-lane avenue flanked by tall trees and five and six story houses. Ahi-Ezer is a Hebrew transliteration, which means "my brother's helper" in English. The school was run by predominately Sephardic Rabbis and had a student population consisting of Jews whose families had originated in Syria. The school had approximately three hundred kids from kindergarten through eighth grade. All of the classes were segregated between boys and girls; the two sexes rarely interacted with one another. Ahi-Ezer had a very stringent dress code. Boys were required to wear Yarmulkes or skull caps to cover their heads. Even though covering one's head was neither a Biblical nor Rabbinic law, this relatively recent practice had grown in importance and the school required it.

I asked my Rabbi, "Why are boys required to wear Yarmulkes or head coverings while girls aren't?"

His quick pronouncement was, "Men need to be constantly reminded they are not G-d and someone is above them at all times, women don't need to be reminded."

The boys also wore Tsisit under their shirts. Tsisit were fringes or tassels worn on the corners of a rectangular piece of white cotton cloth with an opening in the center through which the head can pass through. This was an ancient custom and was probably a form of tribal identification which separated Jews from gentiles. Jews were not allowed to sell a garment with fringes to a non-Jew without removing the tassels first. The purpose of the fringes was to remind

Jews of the 613 commandments. The garment had threads that were doubled back at each of the four corners. Four corners doubled back are mathematically represented as $4 \times 2 = 8$. There were 5 knots on each of the tassels ($8+5=13$). The numerical sum of the Hebrew letters in the word tsisit is 600, and through the magic of Jewish math, the garment in total represents the 613 commandments.

Girls had to wear very modest dresses. Skirts were supposed to cover the knee. The blouses they wore had to cover their shoulders and most wore full-length sleeves in both summer and winter. Neither boys nor girls could wear jeans. The slacks boys wore would often have holes in them since they were not as durable as jeans.

The school had no playground per se; it only had a concrete area where the kids would play handball off the school's building walls or stoopball off the stairs to the front of the school. Boys would have recess at a different time from the girls, so we never got to see who was better at these games.

Even though my father did not have the money at this time to send us to a private school, the school accepted my sister and later me, and waived all tuition charges. When my father finally became more financially stable, he would not only pay our tuition, but would help subsidize other children who could not pay. I always thought the school had an appropriate name. Ahi-Ezer always had a policy of accepting anyone who wanted to attend regardless of their ability to pay.

The teachers at Ahi-Ezer were Rabbis and the focus of the learning was on Hebrew, Judaic Studies, and Torah or Bible. Secular subjects like English, Math, and U.S. History were not their priority. Probably because the Rabbis were not proficient in those subjects themselves.

The fact I was fluent in Hebrew, since I spoke it at home, made me a teacher's pet. The Rabbis would always point to me and say,

"Look, Gil gets it, and so the rest of you have no excuses." I really felt bad for my class; I had an unfair advantage, Hebrew was my first language.

Hebrew is a very difficult language to learn. It has an entirely different alphabet; it is written from right to left, and has grammatical rules and sounds are totally alien to the English language. When you say a word like Chanukah, you need to act like you have a hairball stuck in your throat and you are trying to clear it in order to get an approximation of what the CHA is supposed to sound like. The language has a lot of guttural sounds in it, which do not exist in English. Americans usually have bad accents when they learn a new language like French or Spanish, but in Hebrew, even when they get the word right, the pronunciation is often so far off that most of us who are fluent can't quite understand what they are trying to say.

My sister was an exact opposite of me when it came to school. She lived in the same house, she heard my parents speak the same Hebrew I heard, but she was one of the worst students Ahi-Ezer ever had. Vered was always in trouble and just couldn't stand school. I don't know how many times I would walk down a hallway and see her standing in the corner of a classroom looking at the wall as a punishment for something she did. Often the classroom she was standing in was a few grades below where she was supposed to be and the younger kids in school seemed to know her better than her own classmates.

When Edna joined my sister in Ahi-Ezer Yeshiva it was like adding gasoline to the fire. The two of them together, in the same class, was more than any poor Rabbi could possibly handle. They were nicknamed the "Vilte Chias," Jewish for "Wild Animals." Vered and Edna would feed off of each other and would often try to see who could make the other laugh first. During her Yeshiva years, Edna was a lot like Olive Oyl, the character in the "Popeye the Sailor" cartoon strip. She was always the damsel in distress, had olive colored skin, long dark hair, was tall and skinny, and had enormous feet. Edna's arms and legs seemed to grow faster then the rest of her body, which would explain why she was klutzy. If she reached out for drink her long arms would often knock over everything else in front of her, usually right on Vered, who was always sitting next to her. Edna would trip over herself walking down a hallway or up a set of stairs, or she would kick things with her big toe, which must have been broken during most of her adolescence. But Edna's short awkward phase would soon be eclipsed by the beautiful and exotic women she would grow up to be. All of my male friends would literally fall over themselves just to be around her by the time we were in high school. My aunt seemed to enjoy getting in trouble in Hebrew school. When Edna got her first bra, she decided to show her religious studies class her new bra by swinging it over her head. The Rabbi, who taught the class, thinking she was disrobing, almost had a heart attack and ran out of the room as fast as he could to ask for help from a female secretary.

I remember one Rabbi telling me, "When G-d was giving out brains, he must have given your aunt's and sister's portions to someone else." Edna and Vered were pleased when they just passed a class. I have a feeling the only reason they passed was the fact the Rabbis didn't want to deal with them for another year had they failed them. I don't know how many times I would see one or both of them running down the hallway with a Rabbi in hot pursuit yelling "Vilte Chais, Vilte Chais." My parents spent more time in the principal's office than any other parents I know.

10. King Achashverosh

Purim is one of Judaism's most fun holidays. You get to play dress up and eat doughy triangles filled with prunes and poppy seeds. The triangles are supposed to represent the ears of the villain in the story, Haman, and are called Hamantosh.

Ahi-Ezer Yeshiva was putting on a Purim play and I had the role of King Achashverosh. My Emmah could never help me with my English, math or social studies homework, but when I needed something where she was able to help, she would often stay up all night to make certain that I had the best she could possibly provide. Mom hand sewed the most elaborate King Achashverosh costume anyone had ever seen. She made me purple silk pants, a gold silk shirt with a purple collar that was turned up, and a black vest with gold trim fringes I wore over the gold shirt. My shoes were covered in purple fabric and were filled with cotton in the front tip and were curled up and pointed like those of the Wicked Witch of the West's in the "Wizard of Oz." She also made me a golden royal crown and scepter, and she drew this huge Salvadore Dali like mustache on my face. I looked like Ming the Merciless in the Flash Gordon comic book series. Even though I was the one on stage performing, my mother was the real star of this play.

The story of Purim was set in Persia two thousand three hundred years ago. We read the Scroll of Esther which recounts how a seemingly unrelated series of events are interwoven together and results in the saving of the Jewish people from annihilation. King Achashverosh throws a huge six-month long party and his queen, Devashti, refuses to show up for it. So the king has his queen eliminated, which is probably where Henry the VIII got the idea of eliminating his wives. Achashverosh then replaces his queen with Esther, who secretly hides her Jewish identity. Esther's uncle Mordachai uncovers a plot to assassinate the King, which obviously puts him in the King's good graces which comes in handy when Haman, the kings' top advisor, issues a decree to have all of the Jews killed. Esther gets the decree reversed, and Haman ends up hanged on the gallows he built for Esther's uncle. Mordachai then becomes the King's prime minister.

What's interesting about this story, and most Jewish tales for that matter, is that G-d doesn't take credit for his work. His name doesn't appear even once in the Scroll of Esther. His hidden hand is obviously there, but his name isn't. In the story of Exodus in the Passover Seder, the main character Moses' name appears only once, and in general passing in the entire story. We often achieve great things in life, and it is an unseen hand that often helps us; in my early childhood, that hand was my mother's.

11. Oz

The summer of 1969 I asked my parents to go to a camp that was putting on a production of the "Wizard of Oz." I got the part of the Tin Woodsman. This time, though, the costume was not made by my mother, but by the camp counselors who were putting on the play. My entire costume was constructed out of flimsy, silver-colored poster board. To make the arms and legs they rolled up the poster board into tubes. They then taped them together and cut them to the length of my arms and legs. My torso was also wrapped in this same material. The camp staff made what looked like a silver barrel and hung it over my shoulders with straps. The problem with this costume was it had no arm or leg joints. I had no knees or elbows. I could not walk up or down the steps leading to the stage. When I needed to get on stage someone had to carry me and lift me up onto the stage and carry me off the stage when my scene was done. When we did various song and dance numbers like "We're off to see the Wizard" and "Follow the yellow brick road," I had to hop around the stage looking like the Mummy. I can recall the laughter in the audience even before I had the chance to utter a single line. All I had to do was try to move on stage, and the audience would break out in hysterics.

But there was something special about the "Wizard of Oz." It was so well written on many different levels. When a certain line in a play resonates with truth it has a way of embedding itself into your memory. I can still remember these lines....

"I don't know enough," replied the scarecrow cheerfully. "My head is stuffed with straw, you know, and that is why I am going to Oz to ask for some brains."

"Oh, I see," said the Tin Woodsman. "But after all, brains are not the best things in the world."

"Have you any?" inquired the Scarecrow.

"No, my head is quite empty," answered the Woodsman, "but once I had brains, and a heart also; so having tried them both, I should much rather have a heart."

-The Wizard of Oz

L. Frank Braun

12. Naturalized

There are only two ways one can become a citizen of the United States. You are either born a U.S. citizen or you become a naturalized citizen. Naturalization applies to those who are legal permanent residents for at least five years, are eighteen years old or older, and have good moral character, (whatever that means).

As part of the process of becoming an American, my parents needed to take an oath of allegiance to this country and renounce their loyalty to their native country. However, giving up one's allegiance to a country of origin did not mean one needed to give up its citizenship. My mother and father would be dual citizens and they would retain their Israeli citizenship. Many countries allow dual citizenship. Australia, Britain, Canada, and Israel allow it. As Americans we would not be allowed to defend Israel at times of conflict with the United States. Since the United States was Israel's main and at times only ally, this was not a very likely event. I think the only time the allegiance issue ever came into play was during soccer matches. My father always quietly rooted for Israel, but I doubt that would have been considered a national offense.

Right after the fifth anniversary of my parents' becoming resident aliens, they applied for citizenship. In order to apply you had to have your fingerprints taken at an authorized facility as well as obtain two photographs of a specified size. Then it usually took six to eight months before you were given an interview, at which time you took an oath and were asked ten questions out of a list of one hundred possible questions on U.S. history. At the interview they asked you what name you wanted on the certificate. Remarkably, it could be anything you wanted. My father and mother now had another opportunity to have additional legal documents with names that were different from all of the previous documents they already had.

My parents tried to make an appointment for the photos and fingerprints, but the place they chose would not take appointments. They had to wait in a long line for several hours until their names were called. My mother was asked to remove all jewelry for the photos and then they tried to take her fingerprints. She could not keep her hands still and the fingerprints were rejected. The prints needed to be perfect and they had to take them over again. My parents must have been very nervous, the photographs on their citizen papers look like they were deer caught in the headlights of a speeding car. After completing the photographs and fingerprints they were required to submit all of the applicable government forms. They dropped them off at the I.N.S. office with a check for the application fee. The line at the Immigration and Naturalization office went all of the way out the door and around the building. It seemed as though half of the planet wanted to be American.

After thirteen months the long awaited letter came with the interview schedule. My father and mother's interview was set for the next week and they had little time to prepare for their test. Luckily it wasn't a very hard test. It consisted of only ten questions. The test required of an immigrant to be a citizen of the United States was far easier than the test given by the Department of Motor Vehicles in order to drive a car. But tests were not my mother's favorite pastime and she was concerned about this one.

The day of the interview finally came. My parents arrived early. The office was packed and people were nervously waiting their turn to have the exam administered. Several hours passed until finally my father, and then a few minutes later my mother, were both called up to the front desk. The first thing the interviewer did was to make them pledge to tell the truth, the whole truth and nothing but the truth. He then went through every line item on their application forms to make certain there were no errors before he began to administer their exams. When I looked through the various family documents I found my father's study notes for the test.

My father needed to know "Who were the U.S. Senators from the State of New York?"

"They were Jacob Javitts and William F. Buckley"

"What political parties were they from?"

"Both were conservative Republicans"

"How many U.S. Senators are there in Congress?"

"One hundred."

My mother was asked, "What colors are the American flag?"

"Blue, white and red"

"How many states are there in the United States?"

"Fifty."

Remarkably, both my parents passed their interviews and were given a swearing-in date. The Oath Ceremony was on a Friday. They were told to dress appropriately for the occasion. When they arrived at the building for their naturalization ceremony they each got what looked like a wooden lollipop stick about ten inches long with a piece of fabric stapled to it. They were handed the most powerful symbol in the world, a small American flag. This represented all that they now had and all that they could now stand to lose. America offered its people more freedom, opportunity and liberty than any other place on earth. As expected, they then waited for the judge to come in. When he finally arrived, they all stood and sang the national anthem. They listened to the judge speak about the forty or so countries represented by this group and how each had a different and unique story to tell. Finally, they recited the Pledge of

Allegiance, were given their certificates and the judge said the magic words they were all waiting for, "You are all now Americans."

It seemed that the key test to becoming an American was learning patience. Most Israelis find that test to be one of the most difficult skills to learn. Clearly, the privilege and responsibility that came with being an American was worth the wait. When our parents became citizens on August 12, 1969, Vered and I automatically became citizens too. Becoming a citizen was a big deal. This great country was accepting Jaffa, Harry, Vered and Gil. They were actually letting my family become members of the "American Club." Citizenship meant we belonged here (most of the time), we fit in (in our own unique way), and this was our country too.

13. Driving

It's 1972. I'm sitting in the Department of Motor Vehicles in Brooklyn New York, nervous about taking my first written driver's test. I'm ten years old. No, New York did not lower the age of taking driving tests to ten. If you were an immigrant who did not speak good English and for which a written test was not available in the language you spoke, you could bring in a translator to help interpret the test. The test was offered in Spanish, French, Italian and German. Hebrew, at that time, was not a language they offered the written test in, so I was brought in as the interpreter. The thing is I was both the interpreter and the real test taker. I was always a good student and my family realized I could memorize a lot of information at a very young age, so they asked me to review the driving regulation manuals and take the test for them. I will not mention who the family members were, because some of them are still driving today. I am proud to say one family member even became a New York City taxicab driver.

As an adult, I want to apologize to the State of New York for my family's driving abilities. It seems to me most New Yorkers ignore road rules anyhow, and the fact my family is not familiar with the driving rules is hardly ever noticed. I am also happy to say New York now offers the written test in Hebrew, and I think I may have had an inadvertent part in New York's decision to translate their exam into Hebrew. The test back then consisted of a DMV employee who had a blank look on his face administering questions verbally to me, and I would then supposedly translate both the question and answer.

The first question was:

What color and shape is a Regulation Sign?

a.   Yellow and diamond shaped with black lettering

b.   White Rectangles with black lettering or symbols

c.   Red and White with Red Letters

d.   Blue and white symbols

e.   Both A and B

f.   All of the above

I would then ask my family member what was for dinner tonight in Hebrew; while I pondered the answer, they would then tell me what was for dinner in Hebrew, and I would in turn tell the test-giver in English that the answer was f) All of the above.

He then asked the next question. I thought to myself, I got the first question correct, I was on a roll, and this was going to be easy, until I got the next question.

What best describes what you must do at a Stop Sign?

a.   Come to a Full Stop

b.   Yield the right of way to vehicles and pedestrians in or approaching the intersection

c.   Go when it is safe

d.   Red with White Letters

e.   All of the above

I followed the same procedure as before, I would ask the person in Hebrew what they were going to do later today, they would give me the answer in Hebrew, and I would give the answer to the test giver in English—"All of the above."

The problem arose because the answers to both the first and second questions were "All of the above, but the answers in Hebrew the test-giver heard my family member give sounded different to him. Of course they sounded different; the first answer dealt with what I was having for dinner, and the second answer dealt with what we were doing after the test. The test-giver was becoming suspicious and had this look on his face like something was not right here. This required me to think fast on my feet. I told him although the first and second answers were both "All of the above," the first answer was item F on the list, and the second answer was item E. He must have been thinking I'm talking to a kid, how could he know what the driving regulations in the state of New York are, and so he continued to administer the test. This time he decided to ask one more difficult question where the answer was "All of the above," and it was E on the multiple-choice answers to hear if he got the same answer as before.

What does it mean if an edge line slants toward the center of the road?

a.   The sidewalk is wider ahead

b.   The road is narrower ahead

c.   Both A & B

d.   Drive cautiously and follow the edge line as it slants

e.   All of the above

Now I had to tell my relative to give me the same answer to the question I asked earlier regarding what we were doing after the test was completed. They gave the same answer, and he seemed satisfied, until I realized he was going to take an entirely different approach with the next question.

The next question he gave me required my family member to show him, with their own hands, what the various hand signals were before you made certain road maneuvers.

What is the hand signal for stopping or slowing?

Now this became a game of Charades, in lieu of just asking a question and giving him an answer, I had to describe to my family members what I wanted them to do with their hands to make the appropriate signal.

How do I tell them to put their left arm out, but it has to hang down? The DMV test giver must have wondered why a nine-word question required a fifty-word translation. I told my relatives to stick their left hand out and hang it down. They had no clue at what I was getting at. They would stick their hand straight out, then they would point it straight down. I would then say "NO" "NO" in Hebrew "LOH" "LOH" and describe that it needed to be bent or hang down. The test giver could obviously tell I was giving them instructions, but he must have thought this was too funny to stop and kept these questions up.

He then asked the fifth question:

What is the signal for a left-hand turn?

I thought, this is good, this one was easy, all they had to do is put out their left hand in a stretched out manner. But not my family, when I told them to put out their left arm and stretch it out they decided they also needed to wave it wildly at the test giver. I almost lost it. To my surprise after twenty more such questions, I passed my first driving test. Luckily, the next few times I took the test, I had a different DMV employee. I also showed my relatives how the hand signals are supposed to work before we came to the DMV office in case those questions came up again.

The problems associated with not knowing all of the road rules and what the signs mean became very evident shortly after various family members took to the road. One day, my father needed to go to a meeting in Manhattan and my mother agreed to drive him. He was running late, so he told her to drop him off in front of the building while she would try and find a parking space. A few minutes later she met up with my father who was astonished at how quickly she was able to find a parking space.

He told her "I hope you didn't park in a very expensive spot, you know we are tight on money right now."

She said, "You will be so proud of me, I found a great parking spot and it didn't cost anything."

Dad then asked her, "Where in Manhattan did you find a free parking spot so quickly?"

She then responded, "I parked in a Two Way Zone".

It took my father a minute or two to register that there is no such thing as a "Two Way Zone" and mother had parked in a "Tow Away Zone". By the time they got down to the car, it was already towed.

My mother wasn't the only one who had problems with the road rules; my grandmother Ahuva would often request assistance while she was driving. She would drive with both hands on the wheel, often hunched over the wheel like most grandmothers, and would often ask us what she should do when she saw certain signs. Ahuva was primarily responsible for driving Vered, Edna and me to Ahi-Ezer School everyday. She also worked in the cafeteria, so it was convenient. Edna would often sit in the front of the car, while Vered and I would sit in the back of the car. One day my grandmother came to a stop sign and for some reason she could not see oncoming traffic from the opposite side of the street. She asked

Edna to let her know when the way was clear and when she could go.

Edna then loudly said, "Go!"

My grandmother then said "What?"

Edna said "Go-Now!"

My grandmother immediately hit the brake and stopped the car. She then pulled off a rubber flip flop from her foot and began beating Edna on the side of the head. She kept saying, "Why do you first tell me GO and then you tell me NO? Are you trying to kill us?"

My sister and I intended to come to Edna's defense, really, I mean it, but we couldn't speak because we were snickering, snorting and laughing so hard. Edna took a good five-minute beating until we could finally tell my grandmother Edna said "GO-NOW" not "GO-NO".

Another driving habit the women, in particular, in my family had was to accelerate whenever they saw a red light up ahead. I never quite got why they did this. They would see the light about to change to red. They would then hit the accelerator causing me or anyone else in the car with them to be pressed back into their chair, only to hit the brake as hard they could when we got to the red light. This caused the passengers to be whipped back and forth in their seats. The women would then act like they wanted to just get up close and confirm the light had really turned to red. I still suffer from neck and back problems due to the fact I had to be driven by the women in my family in my childhood. The Americans who give immigrants a hard time for their driving abilities are probably basing that opinion on my family's driving habits alone; it's really not fair to all of the other immigrants.

14. Avenue X

My parents purchased their first home in the United States in Brooklyn, New York on Avenue X and 72nd Street. The home was only twelve miles from John F. Kennedy Airport in Jamaica, New York. It was in the direct flight path of the planes taking off and landing at Kennedy. If you were outside when a plane was about to land, you could actually feel the engine's roar throughout your body. We used to play a game as kids where we would guess what airline a plane was when it was still at a distance. Then when it flew was just over our heads we would confirm the airline by reading the logo painted on the tail. Once you were inside the house though you didn't notice the noise much or it's also possible over time we lost enough of our auditory faculties we just couldn't hear it anymore.

Our house was a red brick duplex with white trim of the kind Brooklyn was famous for. It was a home that was attached by a single wall to the neighbor's. Unlike Borough Park, this neighborhood consisted of two primary immigrant groups, Jews and Italians. The neighbors, with whom we shared a common wall, were Italian immigrants. Sal, was a fisherman, whom we would rarely see. He went to work before the sun came up and would work late into the night. He sold his fish at the bustling Fulton Fish market on South Street. Sal always had the combined fragrance of fish and the sea. He wore rubber boots and soiled sneakers that were left at the threshold of his entry door. Three in the morning was midday for him. None of the immigrants in our neighborhood were afraid of hard work and Sal was typical. He had a wife, Vonda, who couldn't speak much English, as well as three sons, Sal Jr., Anthony and Michael. Like most Italians in the neighborhood they were devout Catholics. As you looked into Sal and Vonda's house you could see a knee-high ceramic statue of the Virgin Mary. Italians and Jews had always historically gotten along. We were both close to our immediate and extended families, liked to eat a lot, talked with our hands, and were generally really loud and hot tempered.

Our duplex was three stories tall. When you came in the front door you would need to go up four steps to get to the main floor, which was the middle floor. As you stepped into our home, the first room to your left was what we called the Museum. It was the living room our Emmah never let us into. She had these custom-made pieces of furniture that we were never allowed to touch. The sofa had an orange, yellow, and green paisley patterned fabric and an Asian style wood trim base painted black. It also had large black wooden horns projecting upward off the back of the sofa. It was uniquely Jaffa's style. She combined Asia with the Wild West and covered it in a 1960's revolutionary fabric. It was as though Chairman Mao had gone on a psychedelic trip to Wyoming. Mom also had an oblong glass coffee table in front of the sofa. In the corner of the room she also had a green velvet, rocking, love chaise. It was shaped like a wave, a big green velvet wave. People, who did not know it rocked, would often sit on the front edge of the love chaise, and it would then lunge forward throwing them onto the floor. This chaise was a great source of amusement for my sister and me. We never told our guests this was a rocker love chaise, and we knew they would shortly be sitting on the floor. The walls in this room were covered with various pieces of artwork that consisted of everything from Picasso to Chagal lithographs. If my sister and I ever wanted to irritate Emmah, all we had to do was step foot in that room.

The next room over was the formal dining room, which was far more traditional than the living room. It had a long dark mahogany table and eight chairs and a beautiful crystal chandelier. The kitchen was the last room on that floor, and there was a balcony off the kitchen overlooking the backyard. The kitchen was the room we used the most in this house. There were always great smells coming from mom's kitchen. She learned how to cook as an Ashkenazi from her Bobbeh, and a Sephardi from her mother. We had both Eastern European dishes as well as Middle Eastern dishes served to us as kids. Mom would spice her foods with turmeric, cumin, ginger, marjoram, paprika, ground cayenne red pepper, and cinnamon to name a few. She was never shy about using lots of spices in her cooking. But don't bother asking her for a recipe, because it usually consisted of a little or a lot of this and a little of that. It would be impossible to follow unless you were watching her.

Upstairs we had three bedrooms. The master bedroom over-looked the street out front, my bedroom was in the middle, the third bedroom was my sister's room, and it over looked the back-yard.

When my Emmah and Abbah would fight, which was often, I would have to sleep in my parent's room with my Abbah. Emmah would sleep in my room. Abbah had a snore so loud it shook the house. He snored like a jackhammer. I would try to sleep by sticking my fingers in my ears. When that didn't work, I would try putting on my headphones from my stereo. Thankfully they covered my ears entirely and muffled the noise enough for me to get some sleep. How my mother managed to sleep in the same room with my father is a mystery to me. When I would wake up groggy the next day, I would yell at Emmah and say, "You married Abbah, not me. Why am I being punished every time you have a fight?" I was always relieved and happy when they made up.

My room was small, but it had a large bookcase that went from the floor to the ceiling. When I wanted to hide from everyone, I would climb up the bookshelves and lie on the top one. When someone went into my room, they couldn't see me. I would lie still like a snake on a tree branch. Someone could be right next to me and not know it. My mother would go looking for me throughout the house and but I would just lie there quietly until I could tell she was starting to freak out. Then I knew I had better answer her, or I would be in for it. I would often play with her mind telling her I was in my room and she just didn't see me or hear me.

Our third level was the basement. We had a fourth bedroom built down there with a shower for our housekeeper/nanny, and the balance of the basement was a bar and game room where my parents used to play poker and throw their parties. The backyard consisted of a large above the ground swimming pool, which took up the entire backyard. It was only about four feet deep. We would often climb up on the balcony off the second floor of our house and jump into the pool. Luckily, no one ever broke his neck. We also had an area for a small dog run along the side of the house not connected to Sal and Mina's home.

Our home wasn't the only colorful thing. When my mother wasn't wearing various animals' prints, like leopard or zebra patterned clothes, she would dress in black and would wear big black capes. Emmah had black glasses shaped like cat eyes with rhinestone studs in the frames. She also liked having very thin curved-shaped eyebrows. Over the years my mother plucked her eyebrows so many times they stopped growing in. She had to pencil in eyebrows where they should have been. My friends were all convinced mom was really Cat Women from the Batman Series. Since they thought she was cool, I never told them otherwise.

This was a great home and it would always be full of people, guests, neighbors, and neighbor kids. The front door was always open.

15. Ralph and Alvin

Directly across the street from our house lived a family with junk cars in their front yard and garbage strewn everywhere. The kids were always running wild, half dressed, and it appeared they lived with only their mother, as we never saw their father. One kid in particular was my childhood nemesis. His name was Ralphy. I would make a concerted effort to avoid this family whenever I could, but sometimes they were unavoidable. Ralphy was a little older than I was and definitely much bigger. I weighed about ninety pounds then. At the age of eleven, Ralphy must have been over a hundred and twenty pounds and was about a full twelve inches taller than I was. I was very skinny and had a neck that looked like my Adam's apple was a Macintosh. I was also short and nearsighted and was no match for this kid. Ralphy used to torment me and everyone else he could. He was a sadistic bully. Kids like Ralphy are only brave when the person they are picking on isn't a match for them. Fear is often based on which person has to look up and which has to look down, and in this case I was the one who was afraid.

Alvin Stern was my sister's first boyfriend. Alvin's family lived across the street on the corner of 72nd. His family came from Cuba. They were Jews who had originally fled from Germany to Cuba, and at some point immigrated to America when Fidel Castro came to power in Cuba. Alvin was a big guy, about six-foot tall, had dark curly black hair, big brown eyes and was kind of skinny, but muscular. One day Alvin saw Ralphy threatening me from across the street, so he ran over to help me out. Alvin was about four years older than Ralphy and was much bigger than he was. He picked Ralphy up and threw him over his head and slammed him down on the concrete sidewalk. Ralphy was stunned, hurt and didn't move for about five minutes. Alvin told Ralphy if he ever bothered me again he would kill him. Ralphy must have believed him, since he stayed away from me from that point on. I learned an important lesson that day when it came to self-preservation. If you were a short-statured kid like I was, having a bodyguard could come in very handy.

Alvin and his sisters liked having their palms read by my mother and loved hanging around our house. I don't know where my mother learned to read palms; I don't recall her attending Fortune-teller University or taking soothsayer classes as part of her higher education. But it did not deter her from telling people she could read palms and people believed she could. She played and looked the part of a gypsy. My mother would read all of our friend's palms and she would usually tell them they would have a long and pros-perous life. It would be very annoying when Vered or I had friends over for they would often prefer to hang out with our mother instead of us. It was tough to complete with a fortune teller, as far as entertainment value went. When our friends left our home, mom would then tell us if she liked them.

Most parents screen their kid's friends by asking them what kind of grades they had in school, or they would meet their friend's par-ents and determine what kind of household they came from, but not our mother. She used palm reading as her primary screening tool.

When I went back to Brooklyn to visit my cousins, Jerry and Lily Mossberg, who purchased our childhood home on Avenue X, I was told that Ralphy was serving a life sentence at Riker's Island for murder. Ricker's Island is North America's largest prison; it has a prisoner population approaching 15,000 people. Ricker's is often referred to as New York's Sixth Borough. I can't help but think that I could have easily been this lunatic's victim. You learn very quickly growing up in New York that when someone threatens your life they really mean it.

16. Gemini

Gemini's are allowed to have two natures according to the astrologists, and my mother was a Gemini. Her moods could change with the weather, the rising and setting of the sun, and with the ebb and flow of the tides. Manic-depression causes enormous disturbances in the lives of those affected. It often begins in adolescence or early adulthood and may persist throughout ones life. When my mother fell into one of these episodes they would often last for weeks or even months. She would have enormous mood swings between euphoria and depression and between recklessness and listlessness. In the depression phase she would have extreme feelings of sadness, guilt, hopelessness. When she was manic, she would appear agitated and reckless, and her speech was both loud and rapid. There appeared to be several environmental factors involved in triggering these episodes. The stressful and psychologically traumatic events of her childhood combined with her prescription drug abuse were the primary contributors.

One of her doctors prescribed her diet pills. It has since been proven that stimulants, especially those in prescription diet pills, can trigger bipolar disorder. Emmah became addicted to the prescription pills given to her by her doctor. Between the stimulants and the Valium she was taking several pills a day which affected her moods. Depending on whether she was high or low, she would either refuse to get out of bed or smash all of the dishes on our kitchen floor. After a while we started buying cheaper dishes. Each and every fight with my father would result in a new set of china. Our home had more broken dishes than there were in a typical Greek wedding. I am sure she later regretted reacting like she did, but she couldn't help herself, her blood always seemed to flow hot. She also liked taking her anger out on my father's car tires. It was a good thing he was an auto mechanic and was able to fix those tires on his own when she stuck a knife in them. It would take a very special person who could tolerate my mother's shenanigans when she had one of her episodes. Her friend Yaffa Ackerman would often call her to see how she was doing.

Mom would then yell in the background "Tell her I'm sleeping."

I knew Yaffa heard her yelling in the background so I told Yaffa "My mother said to tell you she was sleeping."

Yaffa understood my mother, and she would still call her the next day to see how she was doing. Most people would have been insulted and wouldn't bother with someone who was as difficult as my mom. But those who did make the effort were rewarded by the amusement my mother would offer them.

The drugs available today to help treat this illness were not available back then. The doctors who she went to for help were often the same ones who gave her the drugs causing these episodes in the first place. Our family was at a loss as to what to do. There was no cure for manic-depression.

17. Lily

My youngest sister was the only one who was born in America. She was given a name that did not require any transliteration into English. Lily is four years younger than I am and eight years younger than Vered.

Abbah was elated when he heard my mom was pregnant, but elation was not Emmah's reaction. Lily was not planned, she just happened. My mother had such a hard time with my pregnancy and was feeling overwhelmed. She couldn't handle another child and was also suffering from depression. Dad convinced her it was fate to have a third child and luckily my mother always felt she couldn't fight fate. My father also promised mom he would hire her help and we would get a nanny from Israel who would make certain we would not forget Hebrew.

Lily was a chubby little thing. She had round cheeks and a round face like my grandmother's. She shared a room with Vered in the back of our third floor duplex overlooking the pool in the backyard. With the two girls in that one room I rarely ventured into their space. The girls would often be jealous of the fact I had my own room, but that was one of the privileges of being an only son. It wasn't all-bad sharing a room though, as Lily grew up, she was able to borrow all of Vered's clothes.

Vered cared for Lily throughout her early childhood. My older sister, who was only eight or nine years old at the time, would help feed, bath, change diapers and walk Lily around the neighborhood in her stroller. She nurtured her maternal instincts watching over our little sister and to a lesser extent me. My mother was doing battle with her own demons, and Vered had to step in as a mini mom until we could get help.

It's evident by the time parents have a third child they are so comfortable with the fact they have not caused grievous harm to the first two, they feel they can do no harm to the third. Lily was definitely a third child. I think my parents would have let her juggle chain saws without blinking an eye. No adult was really watching Lily as she was growing up. She would need to learn to survive her errors and outgrow the experiments of her youth on her own.

18. The Nanny

Abbah called his parents and asked them to find us a nanny in Israel as soon as possible. My grandparents interviewed a young girl about seventeen years old, who happened to be named Lily. She was exactly what the doctor ordered. Knowing my mother was obsessed with cleanliness, and given the fact this girl was a hygiene and cleanliness freak, they knew instantly Lily would be a good fit and offered her the job. Our nanny came from a very large family of Sephardic Jews. She was one of ten children. She had no formal nanny training, but with nine siblings, we knew caring for three kids would be easy compared to what she had to do at home. I'm also sure my grandparents stretched the truth a little by telling her we were easy to deal with and caring for us would hardly be considered work.

Lily spoke no English. This was going to be her first trip anywhere and unlike Mary Poppins, she wasn't going to arrive by dangling from her flying umbrella. She would have to board an airplane. According to Lily, she tried to put her fears aside but walked onto the plane on increasingly shaky legs. She quickly took her chair next to the window, and after what seemed to be an eternity the plane started to move. The plane went faster and faster until the runway lights became a blur and then faded as it lifted off the ground. Lily's stomach churned as she took the first glimpse out of the window and saw the land she was from shrinking away below her. But she knew this was going to be an exciting new life. She just didn't know how exciting. Lily arrived in New York in one piece and my parents brought her home where she settled in downstairs in her bedroom.

I remember Lily brushing her teeth incessantly, up to ten times a day, and flossing three times a day. She wanted to make certain she would not lose her teeth like her father did. Lily and my mother got along fine; they both had similar backgrounds and were both disinfectant aficionados. I now had an older and a younger sister named Lily. I liked to play tricks on our nanny. I used to lock her in her shower in the basement for hours. I would also like to hide her stuff and make her look all over for it. I was a terrible little monster. We never felt Lily was an adult who oversaw us, she was just our older playmate.

When Lily arrived in New York she was like an alien who landed from another planet. She didn't know how to speak English, how things worked in the U.S, how to go places or do anything on her own. But my parents sent her to night school to learn the language and by the time she returned to Israel she was fluent in English. Years later she became an officer in the Israeli Army and her primary job was English translation. America opened a lot of doors for everyone who was fortunate enough to pass through them and my family opened that door for Lily.

19. George and Yaffa

My parent's closest friends in New York were George and Yaffa Ackerman. They too emigrated from Israel. When they first arrived in the United States they slept on cots in the print shop they owned. They worked and lived in their shop until they built their business into one of New York's largest print houses.

George was a big man, over six feet tall; he weighed over two hundred pounds and had an enormous presence. Oscar Wilde was quoted saying "Moderation is a fatal thing. Nothing succeeds like excess." George never did anything in moderation and everything in excess was a good thing. He would smoke, drink, eat and gamble like there was no tomorrow. When he came over to eat at our house, I remember him opening the top button on his pants to make room for the food. When we went out to "all you can eat" restaurants you could see the restaurant owners sweating. They knew they were not going to make a profit on George.

He was a big stakes gambler both in his business and personal life. George and Yaffa would play poker at our home at least once a month. When the adults played poker, the kids would often sit behind them observing quietly. If we made any noise or distracted the adults, we were sent to bed, so we usually were like flies on the wall and just watched the action intently. The adults would be drinking, smoking and gambling while we were on the edge of our chairs watching George work his magic through the cirrus cloud of smoke around him. He would flick his ash-tap, tap, tap and lean forward to place his bet as everyone held their breath to see what he would do next. When George started losing he would often change the game. His favorite was having everyone take a one hundred dollar bill from his or her wallet and using the serial numbers see who could come up with the best hand of poker. The best five digits took everyone else's hundred. In the 1970's these were high stakes games and people could make or lose five thousand dollars in a single night. George would bet on anything. He bet me I couldn't hold my breath and swim four laps underwater in our pool without coming up for air. I think I would have drowned myself before I lost that bet. It was the easiest hundred I ever made in my life.

George was the most successful of my parent's friends. He had a successful business, a large home, and drove a Rolls Royce. I had never seen a Rolls Royce prior to George's Silver Spur. Only a small number of these vehicles were hand-crafted in England. Typically fewer than 1,000 were manufactured annually. When we were being driven in the car, there was absolutely no realization of any movement. The wood detailing in the car had the visual appeal of fine furniture, which was obviously achieved by the painstaking selection and matching of the fine walnut burl. You sank into the leather seats and could tell that only the highest quality hides were used. People would look into the car to see what famous person was sitting in the back. When George drove up to a restaurant, his car would always be front and center just like George always was.

George had a son, David who was my age, and three daughters. Two of the girls were older than I and one was younger. David and I have known each other our entire lives. Our parents were friends from the time we were infants. We would emulate our parents and when they played cards so did we. A typical poker game would leave me with bags of David's pennies. When we get together now, I make certain I always pick up the tab for dinner. I really do owe him and it's just a payback from our childhood. David and I also liked taking things apart to see how they worked. We would build things together like go-carts. This was especially annoying to my parents because the parts for our construction projects would be scavenged from our household appliances. My parents were never able to move our barbeque again after one of David's visits because the wheels were on our go-cart.

We always enjoyed having the Ackermans over. The house would come alive when they visited. It would fill with laughter, smoke, loud voices and lots of food.

George's business kept growing to the point that the employees in his shop decided to unionize. George couldn't understand how a business he built by living and working in it twenty-four hours a day and using every cent of capital he had, now required him to speak to a shop foreman when he needed to talk with his employees. George decided he would rather move all of his printing equipment and start over again than allow the union to take over his business in New York. The Ackermans left New York and moved to Florida in 1973.

20. The Godfather

On October 6, 1973, the Jewish holy day of Yom Kippur, in a surprise Arab offensive, Egyptian forces attacked Israel from the Suez Canal in the south and Syrian forces attacked from the Golan Heights in the north. After huge early losses, Israeli counterattacks quickly pushed the Syrians back into Syrian territory in the north and outflanked the Egyptians in the south. It was President Nixon who helped Israel by replenishing Israel's armaments that were lost at the beginning of the war. OPEC (the Organization of Petroleum Exporting Countries) responded on October 17 by imposing an oil embargo on the U.S. while increasing prices by 70% to America's Western European allies. The shock wave was almost immediate. A severe recession hit America and much of the Western World. Gasoline lines snaked their way around city blocks and tempers flared as customers had to wait hours to fuel their cars. Gasoline prices went from .30 cents a gallon to $1.20 a gallon at the height of the crisis. President Nixon banned gasoline sales on Sundays and extended daylight savings time. Gas stations were asked to hold their sales to a maximum of ten gallons per customer.

Abbah's gasoline station was no different than those around the country. Gasoline lines snaked around it for over a mile during the day. Tempers were frayed and it became dangerous to sell gas in New York. My father purchased a .357 magnum, which he took to work. Dad was approached by a group of mobsters. I think the boss was named Tony Gepetto or something that approximates that. My father must have thought they were going to extort or hurt him, but they did neither. Gepetto and his crew wanted my father to fuel their cars a few hours before he opened the station to the general public. If Abbah had said no to them, I don't think he would be here today. He obviously agreed to go to work two to three hours early and sell them the gasoline. They told my father they would owe him one, and if he ever needed anything from them all he had to do was call. My sister and I had an argument with our next-door neighbor's kids, shortly after Tony told my father he owed him one. The neighbors on the other side of our house started doing nasty things to our property like throwing nails in our pool and damaging our fence. My father tried to talk to the kid's parents, but the parents told my father it wasn't their kids who were doing anything, and to get the hell off their property. So dad called in his favor from the guys he sold fuel to. He asked them to see if they could talk the neighbors into stopping this destructive behavior. After the mob visited our neighbors, no one in the neighborhood messed with us. They didn't even dare to park on the street near the sidewalk in front of our house. When they would see my dad come home, people would often run in the opposite direction. I guess word spread like wild fire that my father was in the mafia, which was not true. To make matters worse as far as perceptions went, my father purchased a used black Cadillac limousine with fins. Mom drove the car mainly. I thought it was the coolest ride around. My sister and I would sit in the back and pull down the tray tables and have breakfast on the way to school in it. The image of my mother in black clothes, black cape, and black cat-eye-shaped glasses with rhinestone studs driving a black limousine really had everyone talking. We definitely fit the image of a mob family and people thought dad was the Godfather. Little did anyone know we were more similar to the Addams Family than a Mob Family.

21. A Hairy Business

"I just love animals," my Emmah would often say.

"How hard could it be to groom dogs?"

"I don't have a language barrier with animals"

Emmah was feeling low and was bored staying at home. She decided working at something creative would be good for her. There were no laws governing the grooming profession. Anyone could become a groomer and open a shop with little or no training.

There is a lot more to consider than just loving dogs if you plan on becoming a groomer. Grooming is a very physically demanding job. You are constantly bending, lifting, standing, and moving all day. Not all dogs are well behaved, and getting bitten is a common occurrence. Some dogs have fleas, ticks, lice, and warts, as well as a host of other maladies. The schedule is very demanding. It's not a job you can take home with you, or one where you can leave tasks for the next day. You must complete your work that day, even if you have to work late to get everything done. Your four-legged clients do not always cooperate. Sometimes the dogs are not feeling well when they come to the shop, and after you have groomed and bathed them they decide to poop all over themselves, so that you have to bathe and groom them all over again.

There is really a lot one needs to know to be a groomer. You need to become proficient at clipping, scissoring, proper bathing and blow-drying. Knowing how to handle different breeds and understanding various dog behaviors is also critical. In addition, at the end of every leash is an owner who views their pet as a family member in a fur coat, and these people often love these animals more than the other two-legged members of their family.

Generally shop owners are women who are creative and love animals. Mom opened her shop in Brooklyn about one block from the elevated train tracks. For some reason my parents liked noise in their life; we lived in the flight path of Kennedy Airport and would hear planes roaring over our heads at home, and my mother worked by the F train tracks. She'd hear the trains screeching by all day while the dogs howled and barked in their cages.

My mother purchased the shop, which to the best of my recollection was called either Jo Mere's or Germes. If I spelled Germes correctly, then it is the French word for germs. She purchased a dog-grooming salon called germs. I doubt she ever looked up what the name of the salon meant. The previous owner named the shop and trained my mother.

Remarkably, Emmah was a very talented groomer. Her dogs looked like works of art when she finished with them. The most common dog she groomed was a Poodle, and when Fluffy, Flopsy, or Mopsy left her shop they all had elaborate designs shaved on their heads, feet, backs and tails. I have seen crop circles, which didn't look as elaborate as the design mom scissored onto these dogs. They had perfectly round hairballs shaved at the bottom of their paws, and at the tip of their tails, there mid sections often had original patterns separating their fronts from their backs. Emmah also learned how to trim nails and paint them with nail polish, clean ears, remove burrs, and care for their skin. She became an expert in all kinds of the different shampoos and conditioners that were appropriate for each kind of dog. These animals had a lot more hair product choices available to them than humans did.

I used to love watching my mother dry the dogs after their baths. She would have these enormous hair dryers, which she would put next to the dog that was on the grooming table. She used the Oster

High Velocity Stand Dryer. This dryer came with a metal stand with wheels on the bottom and it had a long arm with an adjustable nozzle at the end of it in so you could adjust the direction of the high velocity hot air that was created by the dryer. This was very similar to the technology used on the Harrier Jet aircraft. Harrier Jets are aircraft with rotating nozzles which, when they are turned toward the ground lift the plane like a helicopter. Mom would take these little dogs, which were held in place by several leashes and restraints, and turn on the equivalent of a jet engine. The dogs looked like they were in a wind tunnel and mom was studying the effect of hurricane velocity winds on their less than aerodynamic bodies. It was very funny to watch their ears flap and their mouths get stretched back into various contorted expressions. When the dogs left the shop you got the sense they walked with a swagger out the door because they felt they looked great. Personally I thought the poodles looked silly. They had pink ribbons in their hair, painted toes nails, and looked like topiary designed by a Disney landscaper. You wouldn't catch me dead walking one of these poodles in public.

People who learned my mother purchased the shop from the previous owner would ask her what kind of experience she had. She couldn't just say on the job training. People wouldn't buy it. So my father looked into entering her into various dog shows with awards for grooming. After they determined this would be a great expense in travel and other costs, Dad asked what kind of awards they get if they win. He was told they receive a trophy and one hundred dollars for some of the closer competitions. This didn't make business sense to him, so he went to the local trophy shop and purchased several trophies for my mom for twenty dollars and he awarded it to her. The trophies only said first place or second place and nothing else on them. They had plastic dogs mounted on marble bases of varying heights. People were so concerned about their status, it was important for them to say they went to an award winning dog groomer. The key was that their dog was clean and looked great when they left my mother's shop, not the awards the dog groomer won.

The one thing I always hated about mom being a groomer was her appearance when she would pick us up from school. It must have been a struggle for her to finish work in time and pick us up; she'd hurry out of the shop with a clump of hair stuck to her bottom or all over her clothes. My classmates would tease me and tell me my mother shed and they would ask me if I shed, too. The hard work associated with running the grooming salon did not eliminate my mother's depression. My father had to post numerous signs on the door telling her customers she was sick when she refused to get out of bed. After this started becoming a common occurrence, they decided to close the shop.

22. The Luncheonette

On 85th Street and 20th Avenue in Brooklyn, just around the corner from my mother's Germes dog grooming salon, was my aunt Zippi's and her husband's luncheonette. My father's sister Zipora preferred to be called Zippi. Like most of the names in our family, Zippi's Hebrew name didn't work in English. Her name in English was Bird. Shlomo, her husband, had a name that was derived from the Hebrew word Shalom, meaning peace, but Shlomo called himself Sam in English. Shlomo was the chef, and when he wasn't cooking in the kitchen, he would have a cigar held sideways in his mouth, clenched tight by his teeth. He always wore his white apron and seemed to permanently have a ladle at the ready in one hand and a spatula in the other. Shlomo enjoyed standing by the sizzling grill or over a large pot of chicken soup when he wasn't taking orders. Zippi was the cashier behind the Formica counter. The customers, who were part of the working class of Brooklyn, would sit on either the swivel barstools or at the few tables the luncheonette had in addition to the counter area. It was a counter full of quirky New York eccentrics. Vered, mom and I would often go over and get soup or a chocolate éclair from the luncheonette and bring it to the dog grooming salon. But Shlomo, with his chopped liver, chicken soup, or cholent (a slow cooked stew of lima beans and beef), would never let us leave his place with just a cup of soup.

But as soon as the customers were gone, Sholmo and Zippi would start their usual repartee. "The soup was too salty and you made a mess," she would say tersely. "You overcharged the Steinberg's and didn't put their order in correctly," he would yell back. Then she would hiss at him to "Stop puffing that cigar smoke." It was a miracle they never bludgeoned each other to death in that luncheonette.

Zipora and Shlomo had two children. Our cousins Nancy and Jerry are called Nesyah and Yitzhak in Hebrew. Jerry was in high school at the time and worked two jobs. In the morning before class he would go to the local fish market and would be responsible for lining up the fish in the display. Then, smelling like fish all day, he went to school. After school ended, he worked at the clothing store on 85th Street across from the luncheonette and sold men's shirts. The clothing business was referred to as the "smateh" business, which in Jewish meant the rag business. Eventually both Jerry and Nancy worked in the smateh business. While still in high school Jerry, who was fifteen years old and over six feet tall, met his wife Lily, who was sixteen and all of five feet standing on her tippy toes. Lily must have liked the smell of fish, because by the time Jerry was nineteen he was already hooked. Marrying young seems to be the norm in our family. My cousin Nancy was a typical athlete in our family. She took just one step out the front door of her house and told me, "I can't go further, I made a move." I asked her, "What do you mean you made a move? You mean you hardly moved." "No," she said, bent over in pain, "I twisted something and can't move." I am certain the shortest known jogging record known to mankind, a single step, is currently held by my cousin Nancy. Jerry and Nancy have always been close to each other and us. We have a shared childhood and speak to each other as often as possible.

23. Vodka, Love and Charlie Brown

We all dream of having pets that are a pleasure to have inside the house, that live as part of the family, walk well, and obey our every command. Well those were not our pets. They say pet owners usually get animals with similar personality traits to them, and in some cases they even look like their owners.

Vodka was our Siberian husky. His breed originated in Northeastern Siberia, which was part of Russia, and he was an endurance sled dog. They are one of the most independent and stubborn breeds you could own. They typically have deep black or brown and white fur and are medium-sized, weighing about fifty pounds, and have beautiful blue eyes. When I walked him the most common question I was asked was, "Is that a Wolf?" Siberian huskies do not bark, they howl. They make a sound something like WOOO, WOOO, and WOOO. They also clean themselves like cats. Twice a year, and more often in warmer climates, they shed their undercoats completely. Hair comes out in clumps, some large and some small. Owning a Husky means you are going to get a lot of use out of your vacuum cleaner and dog brushes. Trying to walk Vodka on a leash was almost impossible. He would just about pull my arm out of its socket when I tried to walk him. I think I weighed about ninety pounds when we lived on Avenue X, compared to his fifty pounds. He would literally drag me through the neighborhood when I kept him on his leash. He was always high strung and would often run away. Vodka would never listen to my calls to stop it or come back. This Husky was very friendly and not suspicious or afraid of strangers, which made him a terrible guard dog. I think if he were offered a treat, he would take an intruder directly to where we kept the valuables. I used to think Vodka was stupid, but my sense now is he knew what I wanted him to do; he just didn't want to do it.

Love was our second dog, and she was a collie. Collies originated in England, or more specifically in Scotland. The word collie came from the Scottish word *colleys*, which referred to dark sheep native to Scotland. Collies are herd dogs; they are great companions, easily trainable, intelligent and beautiful. Love had a light-gold and white-colored fur, her mane was abundant and her coat was very soft. She had bright eyes, which were able to show great expression. Her ears were carried erect, with the tips slightly drooping and she had a long tail. Love weighed about forty five pounds, and was about twenty-two inches tall. Love used to sleep on the edge of my bed every night, and G-d help anyone who tried to come into my room while I was sleeping. My father once opened the door to my room to check on me, and Love just about bit his head off. My father then closed my door in disgust and rarely went into my room when she was there. Love was my dog. I cared for her and she watched over me.

Vodka and Love made a very odd pair. Having a Russian and an English dog made about as much sense as my Egyptian grand-mother marrying a Russian and then an Englishman. The two dogs did not always get along well. Since Vodka shed a lot of hair we often kept him outside in a small doghouse along the side of our home. Love on the other hand slept in my room. I think Vodka was jealous of Love because she got to be in the house more often than he was, but when he was allowed in the house he would run amok and make a mess of things.

Vodka was notorious for digging under our backyard fence and opening the gate and running off. Love would also run out with him when he got loose.

I would then have to roam my neighborhood screaming at the top of my lungs, "Love, where are you Love?"

"Please come back to me Love."

"Love, come here now!"

"Vodka get back here now, I swear I am going to kill you!"

I always wondered why my neighbors gave me such an odd look when I went roaming the neighborhood yelling for my dogs. But I guess if you didn't know those were the names of our pets, you'd keep your children away from us also.

Our third pet in this animal menagerie was Charlie Brown. One day, my mother walked into our house with something under her coat. When she whipped opened her coat like a flasher, she revealed this short, yellow-orange colored animal with a long black-tipped tail. It had no hair around its lips and nostrils, and had white fur around its ears, eyes and throat. My mother had purchased a Squirrel Monkey, and I was told it was to live with me in my room. We named him Charlie Brown. Owning a primate in New York, or in any residential neighborhood, made absolutely no sense, and it's never a good idea to have pets that look like your relatives. These are wild animals and I wish human primates would learn to respect that.

Charlie Brown initially lived in a huge three foot wide by four foot high cage in my room. Squirrel monkeys are active night and day. The only way he would go to sleep at night was when we covered his cage with a blanket. When he was awake either during the day or night he was usually quiet unless he was alarmed about something, then he would let out a loud cry that would startle the hell out of me. Then we would both scream. Charlie had a wide range of sounds he would use to express himself, most of which I understood.

In the wild, squirrel monkeys feed on insects, fruits and berries. When he was little we gave him Enfamil baby formula in a bottle. As he got a little older we gave him fruit, berries, nuts, and vegetables. I would also give him some of my food from the dinner table. He especially liked to eat pasta and popcorn.

Charlie was a wild animal. As he got older, you could not hold him because he would bite you. The only way you could take him out of his coop was to put on special gloves he could not bite through. If he got out of his cage by accident, you would be in big trouble. He was ultra-hyper and would jump and climb on all of the furniture throughout the house and swing from the curtains until you could capture him and place him back in his enclosure. These monkeys mark their territory by a urine wash. He would urinate on his hands and feet, then spread it around. When I realized that's what he was doing, I immediately asked my mother to remove him from my bedroom. Our monkey was relocated to a small room off the kitchen. One day Charlie found a cord within reach of his cage. He pulled it into his den and chewed on it. When we first saw Charlie Brown passed out we were sure he had electrocuted himself. We thought he was dead and immediately took our limp monkey to our neighbor who was a veterinarian. Charlie had just gotten a little electroshock therapy and luckily survived the ordeal. But, after the electrocution incident, we asked the vet if he wanted to keep our squirrel monkey. Thank goodness he said yes.

It was on a snowy December night a few years later that both Love and Vodka were in our backyard. Vodka opened the gate again and they both escaped. We went looking everywhere for them, and we eventually found Vodka roaming around the neighborhood. We kept looking for Love most of that night and could not find her. The next morning we found she had run onto the Belt Parkway freeway nearby and had been struck by a car and died. This was one of the worst moments of my life. I lost my Love; she was my dog, my protector.

24. The Borscht Belt

The Borscht Belt refers to the predominantly Jewish resort hotels and bungalows in the Catskill Mountains in the Hudson Valley in upstate New York. Jewish farmers began building the bungalows in the 1920's in order to make ends meet. They leased them to visitors from the urban parts of New York. It was called the Borscht Belt because of the popularity of borscht, which was served in the resorts.

Borscht was a reddish-purple colored beet soup served hot or cold, usually with sour cream. The word borscht was originally derived from the Russian word borshch, which later became the Yiddish word borscht. Borscht wasn't the only Jewish staple served in these hotels. Gefilte fish, matzah ball soup and cholent were also served, but the names Gefilte Fish Belt, Matzah Ball Belt, and Cholent Belt never caught on like Borscht Belt did.

Gefilte fish is a cake or ball of chopped up fish. It is usually made of white-fleshed freshwater fish, such as carp or pike. The fish is chopped into small pieces or put into a blender and mixed with onions and carrots, celery and sometimes parsley. The mixture is held together with eggs and matzoh meal. It is then boiled in broth for a while. It is usually served cold with red horseradish. The word "gefilte" comes from the German word, which means, "stuffed." Some people also stuff the fish skin in the blender with the chopped up fish. To me this tastes as repulsive as it sounds, and I have never acquired a taste for gefilte fish.

Matzah ball soup is also known as Jewish penicillin. The soup is made up of a very thin chicken broth with several ping-pong ball sized, or sometimes much larger, matzah balls in it. There are two types of matzah balls, floaters and sinkers. Floaters are very soft and light. Sinkers are very heavy and firm. To make the balls you take matzah meal and mix it with eggs, water and schmaltz (melted chicken fat) and some black pepper and parsley. You then bring the chicken broth to a vigorous boil and drop the balls in the boiling chicken broth. It is usually done when the balls float on top of the broth and look bloated, that is unless you made sinkers which are heavier and don't float. Matzah ball soup has actually cured many of my colds and is a standard cold treatment for Jews.

Cholent is a very slow cooked stew of lima beans, beef, barley and potatoes. It is usually cooked in a crock-pot and left to cook for over a day. This dish is a traditional Sabbath meal because it can be started before Sabbath begins and left to slow cook throughout Sabbath. The meat is so tender it melts in your mouth. The problem though lies with the beans. The beans cause the people who eat them to have terrible gas. This is a warning to the general public; don't go to an event where all of the people have just eaten a lot of cholent. If you are then stuck in a small room with them for hours, this can become both a fire hazard and a hazard to your health.

The Jewish concept of heaven comes complete with feasts and banquets. Food is one of the main rewards you get if you were good enough to go to heaven, and the Catskills were as close to heaven on earth as you could get. Since the turn of the century tens of thousands of Jews hungry for great ethnic food, clean mountain air and the American way of vacationing have made their way to these mountains.

The Borscht Belt provided America with a rich supply of comedians, musicians, and performers. Some of the best known comics from the 1950's and 1960's got their start in the Borscht Belt: Jerry Lewis, Danny Kaye, Milton Berle, Red Buttons, Norm Crosby, Henny Youngman, Buddy Hackett and Jonathan Winters to name a few. The hotels also provided legions of jobs to young workers, which financed a lot of Jewish college educations.

My parents decided to have my elaborate Bar Mitzvah party in the Borscht Belt. The party lasted three days and two nights. They invited the Rabbi from our synagogue, all of their friends and family members, and two of my friends, to stay at the Homowack Kosher Resort Hotel in the Catskill Mountains in Spring Glen, New York.

I can't imagine a marketing director or branding specialist today deciding to name a resort hotel the *HOMO WACK*. I am surprised that the various gay and lesbian groups haven't sued the hotel over its name. A hotel name with the words *homo* and *wack* in it is definitely not politically correct. I'm just really glad my parents did not have their wedding reception at the Homowack; I can't imagine having to go through life with a name like Homo.

I had prepared for my Parsha, or Torah reading, by studying for over a year with my Rabbi at Ahi-Ezer. The studying took place after school and lasted until 6:00 or 7:00 PM. I would then take the bus home from Ocean Parkway to Avenue U and walk from Avenue U to Avenue X. Today, I would never allow my child to ride the bus in New York at night alone, but back then my parents did not think twice about letting a twelve-year-old take the bus or train at night alone.

I woke up Saturday morning, the day of my Bar Mitzvah, and I got dressed. My mother made me wear a green velvet tuxedo with a huge green velvet tie and a white shirt. I told her I had never seen anyone else ever wear a green velvet tuxedo, but she wouldn't budge, and she told me it would make me unique. Even though I looked like our green velvet rocking chaise in our living room, I wore what my mother told me to wear. When I wasn't in my velvet green tuxedo, my father and I wore matching light blue leisure suits with dark blue turtleneck shirts. Leisure suits came right out the encyclopedia of bad taste. It was a suit consisting of a shirt jacket and matching trousers for informal wear made out of 100% polyester and it had snap-together buttons. It was sported by lounge lizards across the United States in the 1970's. Think of John Travolta in *Saturday Night Fever* swaggering in this polyester shirt and suit with gold medallions nestled under his chest hair, except I didn't have chest hair yet. Leisure suits became a *cause de ridicule* in the 1980's. Certain New York restaurants went as far as banning them from being worn in their establishments.

My mother wore a purple dress with long purple sleeves with a deep V cut in the front. The dress also had these huge purple feathers sown around the wrists of her sleeves. She also wore drooping three-inch long silver earrings and had three-inch high purple platform shoes. She looked like a purple Big Bird for my Bar Mitzvah.

I read my Parsha, the Torah portion for my Bar Mitzvah and everyone told me I did a fine job. A Bat or Bar Mitzvah is a major milestone is a young Jewish child's life, and I don't know anyone who has had one that does not cherish the memory of his or hers. But what I remember most was looking very unique in my green velvet tuxedo.

Today, the Borscht Belt has shrunk to only a handful of resorts. The teeming roads are now largely barren. The motels, hotels, and bungalow colonies have all since decayed and most are now gone. People must have gotten bored with the old ways, or they have become much more American and no longer desire to immerse themselves in Jewish culture the way they used to.

25. Skipped

My parents received an urgent call from Ahi-Ezer and they had to come and see Rabbi Saul Wolf, our school principal. To my parent's relief, this time at least, it was not something Edna or Vered did. Rabbi Wolf told my parents the school did not feel they had anything to teach me in the seventh grade I didn't already know. They concluded it would be a good idea if they skipped me from sixth grade to eighth grade. The main reason this occurred was due to the fact I excelled in Judaics, the only subjects that the Rabbis cared about, not because I was brilliant in all of my subjects. I was about to skip the seventh grade where subjects like math, English, and history are based on a cumulative knowledge I did not possess, but that did not seem to deter the school from recommending I be skipped. I should not have agreed to being skipped, but what did I know? I was just a kid. Not only was I being placed into a class where I was going to be behind in most secular subjects, I was going to be the smallest, skinniest, and most nerdy kid in the eighth grade.

The eighth grade was the senior class and the top dogs in our school. These kids went from kindergarten through the eighth grade together. I was the new kid on the block and they hated me for it. In addition, teachers had this false perception of my brilliance so they treated me differently from the other kids. I could do no wrong. Everyone, including my parents, thought I must be some kind of genius. I was so afraid everyone would soon discover the truth about me, and I would disappoint everyone, that I studied all the time. If anything, I consider myself a slow learner. I do not easily understand difficult, technical information. What I do have are the two traits all the men in the family have, determination and stubbornness. I would often be up all night studying the material I needed to understand over and over again until it was finally absorbed into my non-permeable brain.

Ahi-Ezer was notorious for letting me do things I should have never been allowed to do. Cantor Meir Levy, who had an incredible voice, made me both a lead and solo singer in our school choir. You have to understand I am tone deaf. I could not carry a tune for the life of me. But I was able to memorize and pronounce the Hebrew words in the songs correctly, and that was good enough for the Cantor.

When we had a school science fair, I asked my father to bring me a car horn from his garage, and I connected it to a car battery. I placed both the horn and the battery in a cool looking box covered in aluminum foil and connected the two with a small hidden switch. I baffled everyone as to what was really in the box. I called this an experiment in collecting sound waves. A car horn is usually mounted inside of a metal hood of a car and is very, very loud when it does not have a metal car frame muffling the sound. Anytime a classmate tried to explain his science experiment I would turn the switch on. The blast was so loud no one in the room could hear anything any one-else was saying. My box attracted a lot of attention and I won first place prize for this dumb idea.

When the Chief Rabbi of the State of Israel, Rabbi Ovadiah Yossef, came to our school on April 27, 1974 all of the activities in our school were suspended. The city street had been closed. Lettered signs welcoming the Rabbi Yossef were proudly strung across the street and in front of the school. Our entire student body stood on either side of the street as an honor guard to greet the rabbi, who finally arrived with a police escort. The assembly program held in his honor opened with words from Rabbi Wolf, and a single student was selected to give a speech on behalf of the student body, me.

I wasn't feeling well the night before and I had a fever, but I prepared most of the night and wrote the speech with my mother's help. I rehearsed it over and over again until it was memorized. The next morning I dressed in my Sabbath best, a white shirt, a huge black velvet bowtie, black pants and a light blue vest. After I finished my speech in front of the entire student body and the chief rabbi of Israel, they had to wake the Rabbi up from a deep sleep. They woke him up in time for me to introduce him as the next speaker. I have a great photograph of me giving this great speech to a sleeping chief rabbi of Israel. Our distinguished visitor did give a very moving speech about the importance of Yeshiva students immersing themselves in their studies and how important knowledge was, and he also displayed his vast knowledge of Torah. The word rabbi means teacher and this was one of our most knowledgeable teachers.

My senior year of elementary school was very painful socially. I was picked on by some of the bigger kids in the class. I hated getting beaten up or being picked on verbally. I hated having my few close friends feel sorry for me when they couldn't help. So I took a page out of my previous experience with bullies and hired the largest kid in the eighth grade to be my bodyguard. My mother would give me fifty cents a day to buy snacks at school. Since my grandmother worked in the cafeteria, I got all of the food I could possibly want, and so I would use these funds for my protection. We only needed to make the point once to my tormentors. My bodyguard slammed the two kids who were threatening me and making fun of me into a brick wall in the playground. They never bothered me again. Bullies are really cowards; they select victims they perceive to be weaker than they are. Once they are faced with someone of equal or greater strength they run for it.

I graduated valedictorian of my skipped class and although my teachers liked me my classmates didn't. It was not easy being in a class where you did not have shared experiences with your fellow classmates and where you were the odd one out.

26. A New Skin

When you make a major geographic change in your life you get to be born again. It's like a snake shedding its old skin and getting a new one. Leaving Brooklyn and moving to the Sunshine State was going to have an enormous effect on all of us. The lush Florida landscape, especially when compared to Brooklyn's treeless one, was striking. This was the "Venice of America" and the "yachting capital of the world." Florida had hundreds of miles of navigable waterways and inlets and an average year round temperature of seventy seven degrees. The constant warmth of the sun and blue skies was now going to be a fact of life, our life.

People came to Florida in waves, Jews, Cubans, Europeans, Latin Americans, beautiful people, and land speculators. Each swell put down its own layer of culture. But behind this sunny facade were many problems. Like most southern states in America, Florida had a conservative population in the northern Bible belt area, which was in direct contrast to the big cities in the South that were liberal and multicultural. While the Ku Klux Klan and people who liked bikes, beer, and guns clung to the panhandle in the North, Miami Beach in the South held a sizable Jewish population. The racial tensions, religious distinctions, the disparity in wealth and various other issues were simmering just below the utopian surface.

When my parents decided to move to Florida we were all elated. My father was tired of the New York's weather. In winter he shoveled snow and worked outdoors in the cold, and in the summer he sweated in the hot and humid acrid air and his clothes reeked of the smell of gasoline year round. My mother had closed down her dog-grooming salon and was looking forward to hanging out at the beach. Vered and Lily were looking forward to tanning their flesh. I was going to be a freshman in high school and had an opportunity to go where no one knew me. My grandmother Ahuva, Aunt Edna, and John also relocated to Florida. John was an avid fisherman and Florida offered him all of the fishing and boating he could possibly want. Edna would join Vered and Lily in their sun worship rituals.

We were all happy about the move, all of us except Vodka, our Siberian husky. He was bred for winter climates, sledding on snow, and living outdoors. This was not the environment a Husky was bred for. Florida's heat and humidity was extremely uncomfortable for him. I think he must have been the only dog from Siberia in the State. If we thought shedding twice a year was a lot for us to deal with in New York we were not prepared for the year round shedding that Vodka had in Florida.

Our home was a single story U-shaped four-bedroom ranch house on Sky Lake in North Miami. It had a light gray stucco exterior and was in an upper middle class neighborhood. When you entered the front door, you could see through the French doors of the family room out to the backyard. The backyard had a beautiful freeform pool surrounded with Chattahoochee stone decking. This stone was made up of these tiny brown and gray pebbles imbedded in concrete, it was appealing to look at, and not as slippery as wet concrete could be. The entire pool area had a huge two story netted structure. You could see through the netting and it worked well at keeping the bugs out, which were always a problem in Florida. Beyond the netting was a large white wooden floating dock my mother had built on the lake. We would often go out there and feed breadcrumbs to the fish.

The Jaffa room in this house was the Jungle Room. On one side we had a clear-coated varnished knotty pine paneling from the floor to the ceiling. Emmah purchased a leopard's head and a deer's head along with several exotic animal skins and hung them all along this wall. The heads used to look down on us with their cold, angry glass eyes. My Emmah claimed she loved animals but could not understand the irony that these creatures were slaughtered so she could use them as a decoration. The thought of a taxidermist cutting through these beautiful creature's tendons and then peeling back their pelts so they could hang as trophies in our living room made me sick. Emmah also moved the green velvet wave chaise into the corner of this room and placed various animal-patterned covers on pillows, which were on the floor. This was the main party room in our new house. She also had several hookah water pipes and a Turkish brass coffee table atop an intricately carved wooden base in that room.

27. Dance of the East

David Ackerman and I would sit on the floor on the zebra and leopard patterned pillows when my mother threw her elaborate Middle Eastern parties. The performer my mother hired for one particular party was about to enter the room. We were two hormonal teenage boys eager to live out our fantasies. This would be the first time we got to see a belly dancer up close and personal.

Sol Bloom, an American promoter, was the first person to coin the term "belly dancer." He was trying to stir up public interest in the "Streets of Cairo" exhibit at the Chicago World's Fair in 1893. He didn't care that this dance was really called "Egyptian/Oriental Dance" or "Dance of the East" in its native Egypt. He just wanted to attract a large crowd of curiosity seekers to ogle these exotic dancers. In 1893 high society women were laced up tightly in their corsets and never showed any skin in public. Things haven't changed much since 1893, because when men hear they are about to see a belly dancer perform they begin to salivate at the thought of seeing a scantily dressed girl move parts of her body in ways most of us didn't know were possible.

Aliza, the belly dancer, had an elaborate entrance piece. The music was loud and strong and had a very consistent drumbeat with Arabic chanting in the back round. This combination of rhythmic, repetitive sound and her body motions led David and me into a hypnotic trance. We couldn't take our eyes off of her exposed midriff. She wore three circle skirts so that when she spun different layers of her skirt showed themselves. The skirt had two leg slits in the front and one on either of her sides. Aliza looked glamorous in her sequins, beads and glittery black and gold fabric. She had a gold coin bra and belt set that jingled as she moved. Her entire rib cage would undulate and then she would do these amazing stomach flutters. She moved her hands above her head, palms pressed together in a prayer position, while she moved her neck to the left and then the right like Barbara Eden did in "I Dream of Genie," and then she used her arms to make snake-like gestures with rippling hand motions. Aliza moved her hips in a crescent shape from side to side and her pelvis shimmied forward and back at various speeds. This was any young man's fantasy. You were the sultan and had this beautiful, partially clothed woman dancing for you. It's a good thing I was lying down on those pillows. It would have been very embarrassing had I been told I needed to stand up in front of other people at that point. My mother's parties always had a great combination of drama and humor in them. But her Middle Eastern parties were always my favorite.

The Berkovichs
Tzvi (Abbah), Safta Alte, Zipora,
Saba Meir, and Esther

The Mizrahis
Aunt Sima, Safta Ahuva and Jaffa (Emmah)

Jaffa Kalir and Tzvi Berkovich

Jaffa and Sarah Kalir (Bobbeh)

Abraham Kalir and Abbah at my bris

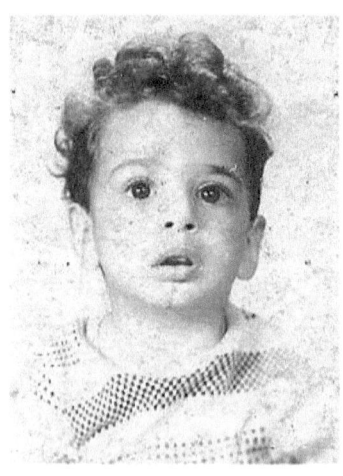

Gil "Happy" Berkovich

Vered, Safta Jamila, and Lily

Gil and Vered

King Achashverosh

Vered, Lily, Emmah and Gil in Brooklyn

Gil, Lily and Vered

Edna, Vered, and Rachel

Vered, Edna, Lily and Gil

Safta Alte feeding me a sandwich

Edna and Vered in our pool in Brooklyn

Aunt Zipora and Shlomo with
their children Jerry and Nancy

Shlomo, Nancy, Jerry and Aunt Zipora

Jerry's Engagement Party
Nancy, Aunt Zipora, Shlomo, Lili and Jerry

Emmah and Abbah and my green velvet tux

Gil and Lily

The Beddeken (Veiling Ceremony)
Victor Kaufmann, Gil, Rabbi Feinstein,
Barbara, and Marilyn Kaufmann

Barbara and Ken Kaufmann

Gil and Barbara

Sarah and Aaron

28. Prep School

While my sisters were sent to public school in North Miami, I was sent to Pine Crest Preparatory School in Fort Lauderdale, a private, independent, all faith, coeducational school. The bucolic forty-nine acre campus on East Cypress Creek Road was about forty-five minutes north of where we lived. I didn't know schools could have that much grass, trees or landscaping. The classrooms were state of the art and had every imaginable amenity. The covered exterior corridors connecting the various buildings were made of red brick and were arched like an aqueduct. At the entry to the school was the Alumni Bell Tower. The bells tolled between classes, indicating one had ended and the next was about to start. At first the sound of the bell tower tormented me. I seemed to be in a perpetual rush going from one class to the next, but now I look back at that sound with fondness. I felt privileged to have been accepted to such a school and I was determined not to disappoint those who gave me this opportunity.

Adapting to this new environment was not going to be easy. It was as though I was told to grow gills and had to breathe underwater. The farther north you went in Florida during the 1970's the more politically and religiously conservative it became. I was a Yeshiva kid from Brooklyn about to attend a school that was advertised as all faith, but had a very small minority of Jewish kids, and after attending classes with only boys, this was going to be my first experience with girls in my class. I would find a quiet corner of the classroom and keep my head down. I was new to town and this school and had yet to find any friend to accept me. My clothes, appearance and personality made me an outsider. I was also pathetic when it came to athletics, and this school prided itself on its athletic programs. I always felt like I was getting in the way, and I finally decided not to compete in sports and just stood by the Coach and talked business with him instead.

Pine Crest started at pre-kindergarten and went through the twelfth grade. Many of the students were lifers and had attended this school as far back as they could remember. The curriculum was extremely challenging, and this time I did not have the Judaic subjects or the Hebrew language to fall back on. We had a nine period academic day. It consisted of six core courses plus physical education, study hall, and lunch. This was a school where one hundred percent of the graduating class went on to a four-year college, an achievement that, if I accomplished it, was going to be a first in my immediate family.

My school day began by getting picked up at about 7:00 a.m. by a Pine Crest school bus. Bus number 17 was the Jew bus. Since most of the Jewish kids lived south of the school, we were all on this one bus. Alan Shuster and Greg Silver were both sophomores when we met. Since they were older and wiser than I was, they became my mentors and friends. Both of their fathers were doctors, and in Alan's case his grandfather was also a doctor. Unlike me, they never had any doubt about what profession they would one day pursue.

Irma, our bus driver, was a southern woman who weighed about three hundred pounds and was about five feet two inches tall. She would yell at us incessantly in a foreign language, or in retrospect, it was possible it was in English, but it was in an accent I never understood. We used to call her Irma the Sperma. It became Greg Silver's and Alan Shuster's and my objective to destroy any intelligence she may have had, and we drove the poor woman into a raving state of lunacy. We would sing, hum, and dance on the bus until she would stop the bus, pull over and tell us she was not going to continue driving until we were quiet. We were called into the office of the Director of Transportation, Mr. Leon Vincenti. In Mr. Vincenti's office, Irma was gnashing her teeth in frustration. When she was angry, her neck turned red and now looked like a fire hydrant. I was expecting an atomic explosion at any minute. When she finally imploded and began screaming at us at the top of her lungs, Greg, Alan and I looked at each other in disbelief and acted like we had no idea what she was talking about. We convinced Mr. Vincenti this particular bus driver was losing her mind. Taking pleasure in other persons suffering is one of man's darker impulses, and teens can be the worst of all creatures when it comes to the enjoyment of the torment of others.

The first class of the morning was in Dr. Jose Perez's Spanish class. Dr. Perez was from Cuba. The Spanish language was nothing like Hebrew. I now understood how difficult Hebrew must have been for my American classmates at Ahi-Ezer. This class required me to study long hours after school and I struggled with the material. Dr. Perez used to call me "Hill." The G in Spanish was pronounced like an H. When I would need to ask a classmate a question, since I was often lost, he would say, "Hill, you get detention for talking in class."

Mr. Anthony Jaswinski taught my English class. I was told Mr. Jaswinski was a Jesuit, which is a Roman Catholic order; and he was taught in a Jesuit school himself. Jesuits were very strict and Mr. Jaswinski was one of the toughest teachers I have ever had. Our class would always begin with a quiz or a test on the short stories we were supposed to have read the night before. The details we were required to remember were things like the name of the street a character lived on, or the color of his shoes or something obscure someone said. We were being taught to pay attention to detail, and if we were going to pass this class, we needed to memorize an incredible amount of minutiae from each story. When it came to grammar and composition, if we had a single fragment or run on sentence in any of our papers, the grade was an automatic "F." The first grade I received on a paper from Mr. Jaswinski was a bold red letter "F" underlined twice. But Mr. Jaswinski would always agree to meet with me after class and go over my paper before it was submitted for grading. He would always answer any questions I had on the reading material as well. I basically lived in his office after school. I had never received any grade lower than an "A" from the Rabbis at Ahi-Ezer, and I was getting an "F" in this class. The contrast between this teacher and my former Rabbis could not have been more striking. At the time, I was certain Mr. Jaswinski's sole purpose in life was tormenting me. In retrospect, I find I owe the toughest teachers I had in school the most gratitude. I learned more from this man than I could have ever imagined. It wasn't easy, but by the end of my freshman year I was able to get my grade back up to an "A."

Mr. Charles Millspaugh was the history teacher. He was the most animated person I ever met. He would often play out the characters in our history books. He would run up beside a student's desk and set a scene by saying something like "You are lying on a beautiful beach, on a bright, sunny Florida day. You are next to this gorgeous babe who whispers in your ear, "Who was Metternich?" What a way to learn history!

Mr. Lansdale taught chemistry class. I would sit in the back of this class with another student named Howard Newmark who was a grade level higher than I was but was new to the school. Howard and I would goof around and once we decided to place a chunk of potassium into an Erlenmeyer flask with a little water. Pure potassium is supposed to ignite when it's combined with water, but the shape of the flask caused enough pressure to build that the glass flask exploded. Howard and I got detention as punishment for this prank and have been friends since.

Our school also had an enforcer. Her name was Mrs. Deideshiemer. We called her Mrs. D. She was part second mother and part rule cop; her official title was Attendance Officer. If you were late, absent or received detention you would have to see Mrs. D. She was always checking, always seeing what you were up to. You couldn't pull anything over Mrs. D. I tried, but since she had already heard every possible excuse, I couldn't get away with anything. She had this sixth sense and could tell just by looking at you if you were up to something. Deideshiemer was always firm, but kind, and I think everyone who attended this school has a special place in his memory for Mrs. D.

From the time Dr. Mae McMillian founded the school in 1934, she promoted tolerance and respect. The problem was that not all of the kids adhered to that philosophy. When I first meet Dr. McMillian she made a point of making sure I knew if I ever had any problems I could discuss them with her, or the principal of the upper school, Mr. Mario Pena, or Mr. George Ring, the Dean of Students. But I was new at this school and even though there was one kid in particular who called me "Jew Boy" and taunted me endlessly my first year, I never went to the administration to complain about him. I would wait for the opportune time to deal with him. I decided to keep a low profile my freshman year and focused on catching up on the academics I was so sorely behind on.

I studied a lot and my parents became concerned I had few, if any friends. I used to lock myself up in my room to study as soon as I came home from school and often keep at it until midnight. I was so far behind the other students; I needed to catch up on eight years of secular studies, which were lacking at my previous school.

My parent's solution to what they perceived was my problem was to buy me an F-18 Formula speedboat. Most parents would be thrilled if their kid studied all the time, but my parent's thought there was something wrong with me. I was told I needed to act more like a kid and not work all of the time. Maybe that was my way of rebelling against my parents. They wanted me to party, so I studied instead. The boat they bought me was eighteen feet long and had a one hundred and eighty-eight horse-power inboard-outboard engine. She had a red V-shaped hull and a white deck and the seats were covered in a soft white vinyl material. This speedboat could glide through the water at up to fifty miles per hour. My mother named her *She's a Lady* from the Tom Jones song that was popular at the time. Since they paid for it, they could name her whatever they wanted as far as I was concerned. I'm astonished to think someone who just turned fourteen years old was given a vehicle with which he could kill both himself and others. It's a miracle I didn't injure anyone with the boat. I was totally irresponsible and would often see how fast I could go and how close I could get to the buoys in the inter-coastal.

The boat did accomplish one of the objectives my parents set out for me. It did help me make friends. I would often go water-skiing or fishing on the weekends, and I would generally not have a hard time finding people to join me.

Alan Schuster, who we called Lippy because he played the trumpet in band and had big lips, and Greg Silver and I went fishing in the ocean off of North Miami. Both Alan and Greg were sophomores, but since we all rode bus #17 and had tortured Irma together we became friends. We shut the engine off, turned on the radio, and drifted for hours with our fishing rods in the water. When we had our buckets full of fish, we decided to head back to shore. When I tried to turn the ignition on, I realized our battery was dead. We were floating north up the Florida coast at what seemed to be at least ten knots an hour. At that rate, we would be in Georgia by the next morning. We waited several hours, but could not see other vessels near us, and my little boat did not have an emergency two-way radio. Greg started to tell Alan that we could survive for days on the raw fish we caught and that sent Alan into screaming panic. After about three hours, as the sun was setting we saw a large fishing boat coming towards us. We were able to signal it and luckily it towed us back to shore. My nickname at school the next day became *Captain Drift*.

Greg and I decided to go into business together that summer. But what kind of business could two teenagers possibly come up with? It had to be both fun and profitable. What we came up with was a company that produced hand painted airbrushed T-shirts, which we sold on the beach in Fort Lauderdale. Greg was a great artist and could draw just about anything, and I discovered I could sell just about anything. We set up shop right on the beach with an air compressor run off the car battery which was connected to an airbrush Greg painted with. We set the T-shirts up on an easel and had two folding chairs, a folding card table, we put on our sunglasses and hats and we were in business.

My sales pitch usually consisted of my showing prospects, which were usually teen girls in bikinis, samples of Greg's work on cotton cloth templates, which we laid out on the folding table. I told each customer that a hand painted shirt was "like a snowflake" or a "human soul." These creations were all one of a kind unique works of art, and were clearly worth the $15.00 we charged for them. Greg and I each made $2,500 that summer going to the beach and spending our day watching the waves and women come and go. What a great country!

29. Cinema

Movies are big business in America. Even though most of the films made today are really terrible, people still pay to go see them. Budgets of one hundred million dollars or more for bad, dumb, and totally implausible films have unfortunately become the norm. I was pretty certain I could make a bad, dumb, totally implausible film for a lot less than a hundred million dollars. So I enrolled in a class called "Introduction to Filmmaking" at Pine Crest, a class that was taught by Mr. Anthony Jaswinski. It was the second year this class was offered at Pine Crest and my friends, who were a year older than I, Greg Silver, Robert Taylor and others, blazed the trail for our class by making successful film spoofs.

Film offered me a new mode of expression. I learned the more I understand something, the more completely I can appreciate it. We were taught about camerawork, lighting, sound recording and editing on 8mm film. Unlike digital video, with 8mm film you had to purchase raw film stock, shoot the film and send it to the lab and wait a week or two before you could view the footage to determine if you had to shoot it again. The cameras also did not have sound on them so after the film was finally edited you would send it to another film lab to put a magnetic sound strip on edge of the film and you would then dub in the sound and music. Even though the film class was costly and time consuming, I loved everything about this class and really learned to appreciate the art of filmmaking.

Movies allowed me to become the center of attention at Pine Crest. We convinced Mr. Jaswinski we should be able to exhibit and charge for viewing our class film project. Since we incurred costs in making the films we should be able to recoup those costs and Mr. Jaswinski agreed. Our first film project was called "Target Cobra." This was a spoof on the James Bond genre. It had George Ackerman's Rolls Royce in it, driven by David Ackerman, various sports cars, an airplane flown by fellow student "Boozer" Rosenbaum, and a car my father gave us that we could wreck on film. We also had the requisite scantily-clad girls who happened to be Vered and Edna. I was agent 00Z, the skinniest near-sighted super hero to ever appear on screen. This was way before the film "Johnny English," starring Roy Atkins also known as Mr. Bean, was released. I always felt they stole our spoof idea for their film, but I have to say, even I was better looking than Mr. Bean. The entire student body saw our films. Some even saw it several times. It wasn't that the film was a great work of art. The students convinced their teachers to let their classes out early so they could see the "Film Class" project; anything was better than being in class. Miraculously, I made a two thousand-dollar profit on "Target Cobra." For a high schooler it was a lot of money.

With the success of my first film, there was no way I wasn't going to make a second film, even though it was not a class requirement. This time, when I told the kids in my class I was making a second film, they lined up to be in it. Some even agreed to help subsidize the cost of production. The second film was a spoof on Alfred Hitchcock's masterpiece, *Psycho*. But instead of the murders taking place at the Bates Motel, we were fraternity brothers who had to stay overnight in a haunted house where a madman named Cedric Eastover murdered his family and disappeared after the murders. If we spent the night there we would be initiated into the fraternity. I can't believe the school let us show what ended up being an R-rated movie. Word spread that this was a very gruesome and violent film, which only made everyone want to see it more.

During the making of the second film I discovered that I could, as director, writer and actor put in the script instructions like "Cute girlfriend kisses Gil before he goes off on his fraternity initiation ritual." Now back in high school, the only way I was going to get a cute girl to kiss me was having it be a movie script requirement. Ann Serrano was my first on screen kiss.

For the violent scenes we used about a gallon of Karo syrup and red food dye to simulate what looked like blood. Our biggest problem was trying to get Saint George Guardabassi, our class president, to stop laughing when we would blow the red Karo Syrup through a small clear tube in St. George's shirt. He said the syrup was cold and he couldn't stop laughing. We had to shoot this scene numerous times to get one shot without him laughing as he dies.

I made more on the second film than I did on the first. I was allowed to charge 50 cents per student. I also realized I could re-exhibit my first film again with new and improved sound. If it got kids out of class they were willing to pay to see it, even a second time.

There is a contagious disease related to filmmaking one gets by being involved in this endeavor, and there isn't any known cure for it. Once a person catches this bug, it becomes really hard to overcome the desire to work in this industry. In my case, the moderate success achieved with my high school films exposed me to the euphoria and the addictive adrenaline rush associated with this illness. I was hooked and determined to pursue it.

30. Dirty Harry

While I woke up each weekday morning to go to an elite prep school located on a beautiful forty-nine acre campus, my father went to work at his dirty, hot and humid, mosquito infested junkyard. Dad decided to acquire this wrecking yard in Florida about a thirty-minute drive north of our home. He knew cars and this was an offshoot of the gas station and repair business.

Big A Auto Parts, as it was called, was on several acres of land. Only a portion of the lot was paved with concrete, the rest of it was just plain dirt. My father had a forklift, a tow truck, a flat bed truck and a crusher on the yard. The employee who lived in a trailer on the site had the requisite mean junkyard German shepard who roamed the property. An old, rusty chain-link fence surrounded the place. The administrative or sales area was only about seven hundred square feet, and always seemed dim. The ceiling light had a glass bowl, which was supposed to be clear but was dark. When you got close enough, you could tell it was full of dead bugs. My father's office was the only one with air conditioning. The conditioned air was from a small window mounted cooling unit, which made an annoying humming sound all day long.

The wrecking yard had rows and rows of empty shells of cars. Some were stacked up on top of each other, and others were already crushed and waiting to be hauled away as scrap metal. There were pieces and parts of vehicles everywhere. Engines, transmissions, drive shafts were strewn out all over the concrete pad. Customers were very impatient. The engines and transmissions were already pulled out of the automobiles and were sitting on the pavement so when the client wanted them they could be delivered without making them wait. This was an automotive graveyard and my father performed the autopsies. He was in the business of transplanting parts out of these wrecked, damaged and rusted vehicles and extending the life of other cars still on the road.

Like most junkyards in the 1970's Dad had at least a thousand parts in his inventory, all of which he kept in his head. He needed to stay up with his part collection on a daily basis. My father did not have a computer-controlled management system. Back then you had to go out in the yard to see if that radiator on the 1971 Ford was still there. Today they just punch the information into a computer and it tells the salesman if the part is in the yard and where it's located. If my father needed a part he did not have, or if another junkyard owner needed a part my father had, they would announce it over a shortwave radio network used by all of the junkyards. The price of the part would be quoted in this cryptic code so the customer who would overhear the discussion would not understand what the part was being sold for. Pricing was a very inexact science in the salvage business. My father would normally start at about fifty per cent of the cost of a new part and then increase or decrease the cost based on supply and demand factors. The customers were very frustrating to deal with. They all loved to haggle and argue over the prices. Some would even pretend to leave in anger only to come back a few minutes later when they saw my father was not going to come down any more on the price.

In the summer of 1977 my father asked me to work with him at the junkyard. He was short-handed, and I was also going to be cheap labor. It was ninety degrees outside. The place was dusty and dirty and smelled like something had died. As soon as I walked out of my father's office, the humidity was so thick it dripped off my face and onto my glasses. I could no longer see through the fog on the lenses. I was covered with sweat, dust and welts from the insect bites.

Both the employees who worked for my father and the customers who came looking for bargains at the yard were generally cheap, rude, foul-mouthed, uneducated hicks.

A customer came up to me and asked, "Hey kid, how much is this Chevy hubcap?"

I responded "Ten Bucks." Looking at the item price on the inventory sheet I had.

The customer then acted angry and said, "Why the hell is this hubcap so expensive?"

I replied, "Sir, the hubcap is only ten bucks, which is less than half the cost of a new one."

He then began to swing his arms and preach at me like a Baptist minister and shout, "Look at this dirty, dusty, bent, hub cap, I might as well buy a new one if I'm going to spend that much money."

I decided go into my father's office and ask him what he wanted me to do. Dad got angry with me for bothering him and this customer for being a pain. He went outside to the yard to where the man was waiting and told the idiot, "Look, stop giving my kid a hard time; the best price I can give you is eight bucks; if you don't like it you can go somewhere else."

The guy looked down on the ground, as if he didn't have the nerve to look my father in the eye, and said "Harry, here's eight bucks; you know I am a good customer. I bought lots of stuff from you over the years."

Well, if he was what a good customer was like, I did not want to even see what a bad customer acted like. I complained to my father incessantly throughout the day. I was hot, uncomfortable, and the insects had already had me for lunch. I had bright red bite marks up and down both of my arms and legs. I hated and was embarrassed by what my father did for a living. The kids I went to school with had fathers who were doctors and lawyers. Their fathers never came home covered in dirt and grease. My father was fed up with my whining and fired me on the first and only day I worked for him. He looked at me with squinting eyes due to the strain of his anger as he barked, "Go home to your mother. I never want you to work for me again". What a relief that was for me. I never wanted to work for him again anyhow. I vowed on that day I would never work at anything requiring me to get my hands dirty.

My father never went to business school. He learned how to run his businesses by trial and error and the seat of his pants. His motivational tools for his employees were very simple. The paycheck was the carrot and being yelled at and getting fired was the stick. My father was a dictator at work. There was only one way you could do things, his way. But I give him a lot of credit for working so hard and for as long as he did. I worked at the yard just one day, but he had to work there everyday. There was so much negativity in his daily life. His customers were brutal to deal with. The heat and atmosphere he worked in was as close to hell as one could imagine. Harry would come home covered in dirt and grease from head to toe. He would often be so exhausted he would go straight into his bedroom and crash on his bed face down. He would fall asleep and start snoring before he even had the chance to remove his dirty clothes or his shoes.

31. Green Eggs

Vered had a friend from Brooklyn who was willing to work hard and was just starting out in life. My father was still short-handed, and I obviously didn't work out as an employee, so Dad hired Vered's friend. He was a Russian immigrant named Yitzhak Schuster, although he preferred to be called Jerry instead of Yitzhak. My parents placed an extra bed in my room, and I had to share my small room with Jerry. Schuster moved down to Florida expecting a lush paradise, gorgeous beaches, and beautiful women in bikinis. Instead he went to work for Dirty Harry at Big A Auto Parts. Jerry was a macho hotheaded Russian. After working with my father all day, he had very little tolerance for my impersonations of his bad English or his tough guy image. One day he took my tennis racket from my bed and heaved it at my head as hard as he could. Luckily I ducked at the last second, and it stuck in my door like the blade of a tomahawk.

It was on a hot Saturday night that summer that Vered, Edna, Jerry and I were watching the 1967 Oscar winning film *Cool Hand Luke* starring Paul Newman. Lucas "Luke" Jackson started the era of the anti-hero in films. This character had heroic qualities but was not in a position where you would normally find a hero. He was in a rural southern prison. Luke committed the petty crime of breaking into several parking meters. When the prison boss tries to break Luke by beating him, his perseverance and charm makes all of the other prisoners respect him. In the film, Paul Newman bets the other prisoners he could eat fifty hard-boiled eggs in sixty minutes without throwing up. Since this was just a movie there was no way the hero was going to lose this bet. While we were watching the film, Jerry decided to let us know how cool he was.

He said, "I can do that," referring to eating fifty eggs in sixty minutes.

I said, "You couldn't even eat half of that amount without throwing up."

Jerry said, "I will bet you anything I can eat twenty five eggs in thirty minutes."

"Without throwing up?" I asked.

"Absolutely," he said.

Vered and Edna knew Jerry could eat a horse. He weighed close to two hundred-pounds and had a huge appetite under normal circumstances. My sister and aunt pressured Jerry to take the bet.

I told Jerry, "I'll bet you three hundred dollars you can't eat twenty five hard boiled eggs in thirty minutes without throwing up."

"You've got a bet," he said.

Luckily for me, Vered and Edna were jumping up and down with excitement, and Jerry was too focused on the task ahead to stop and think a minute about asking me to put the money on the table.

If he had said, "I want you to show me the money," he would have discovered that I had no money. My father fired me on the first day of my job and he didn't pay me for that day either. I had no money. I was certain that I would win this bet. I wasn't worried about what this two hundred pound Russian would do if I lost the bet and he didn't get paid. Then again, I had a hole in my door just for teasing this guy.

Vered and Edna got out a huge pot of water and began to boil it. They then placed twenty-seven eggs in the pot; two more than were necessary just in case some broke. They peeled all of the eggs and put them on a huge plate in front of Jerry. The girls then began massaging his shoulders and stomach to get him relaxed and ready for the two pounds of eggs he was about to eat. My father acted as timekeeper. Dad waited until the second hand reached the top of the dial to tell Jerry to start. Within the first minute Jerry had devoured five eggs. He only needed to eat one egg a minute, and he would easily win. By the second minute he was up to eight eggs. At that rate, the bet would be over in the first ten minutes and "Cool Hand Jerry" would have twenty minutes to spare. The third minute he consumed three more eggs. He was now up to eleven eggs. I began to sweat and thought I was done for. I was pacing back and forth planning my funeral, and I couldn't believe my sister and aunt were rooting for Jerry and against me. So much for blood is thicker than water. By the fifth minute Jerry swallowed a total of fifteen eggs. He only had ten eggs to go and had twenty-five minutes left in which to eat them. I started to tell myself to look at the bright side: he might win, and then he will surely kill me, but at least I knew that eventually the cholesterol from those eggs would kill him too. At some point I would get my revenge.

Jerry was starting to get cocky now. He decided to take a break and walk around the house, but I followed him to make certain he didn't go somewhere to throw up. Two minutes later he came back to the kitchen and said he was ready for more. Ten minutes into this bet Jerry had already shoved twenty eggs down his throat. Then all of a sudden a miracle happened. He slowed down and asked Vered for a glass of water. He began to look peaked, and his Russian skin turned from its normal pale white color to this gorgeous green. Jerry had this very pained expression on his face. His cheeks went from green to bright red. Edna and Vered looked very concerned. I just kept praying he would throw up before he had his heart attack. Then Jerry ran to the kitchen sink and began puking up twenty eggs. It took him as long to regurgitate those eggs as it did to eat them in the first place. I was overcome with joy, and to Jerry's credit he paid me as soon as he finished vomiting. The next day Jerry went to the junkyard to work with my father. When the lunch truck drove up my father purchased two sandwiches. One was for Jerry and the other was his. Dad bought two egg salad sandwiches.

32. The Wise guy

Harry had enough of the junkyard business and decided to sell it in 1978. He took me to the closing of the sale at his attorney's office, thinking I might learn from the experience. I was told to sit quietly and just listen. If I had any questions, I could ask him later. The buyer who walked into the office was a big fellow. His twenty-pound head was totally shaven and he had absolutely no neck. It looked as though a shiny bowling ball was attached directly to his two hundred and fifty-pound steel frame. The guy wore a black T-shirt, black pants and a black jacket. The jacket was so tight around his muscle bulging arms it looked as if he could tear through it just by flexing his torso. Mr. Muscle was dressed in black from head to toe even though it was over eighty degrees outside. The buyer placed his briefcase on the attorney's conference room table and opened it. There were stacks and stacks of Benjamin Franklins in it. He was paying my father in cash. I could tell from my dad's stunned expression he was not expecting cash for the property.

My father' attorney then said, "Would you like a receipt?"

The buyer grinned and responded, "I know where you both live. I don't need any receipts."

After the transaction was completed my father asked his lawyer "Is it legal for me to accept cash?"

The lawyer replied confidently, "As long as the transaction is documented properly, recorded and you pay your taxes, it's legal."

I sat quietly in the corner of the room and watched. I was itching to ask questions, but I didn't dare. I wanted to know …

"Why would a guy who looked like a character from "Men in Black" want to own a junkyard?"

"Why did the Sunshine State seem to attract so many shady characters?

"Where did this guy get his money from?"

"Were cars in South Florida now going to disappear and get chopped up and then get crushed and hauled away as scrap metal?"

"Were there people locked up in the trunk of this guy's car?"

33. A Teenager in Leisure Ville

At the beginning of my senior year of high school my parents informed me they were planning to move to California. Their friends George and Yaffa Ackerman had moved to California, and my parents always seemed to follow George and Yaffa where-ever they went. My family escaped from Czechoslovakia, Lithuania, Egypt, Israel, and New York, and now it was time to leave Florida. The sunshine state did not turn out to be the utopia they had hoped for, and they were now ready for the next perfect place they could call home.

The transition from Ahi Ezer Yeshiva in Brooklyn to Pine Crest in Fort Lauderdale had been very difficult for me, and there was no way I was going to move to a new high school my senior year. Our school had dorms for foreign students who lived on campus, but I wouldn't consider living in the dorms. I convinced my parents to rent an apartment for me so I could finish up my senior year at Pine Crest. I was only sixteen at the time, but my grades were good, I was editor of the year book, I was on the debate team, and was involved in so many other activities there was no way I had the time to get into trouble.

The apartment we found was in a pleasant residential neighbor-hood. It was a low maintenance building, and the community had a lot of amenities, including golf, tennis, swimming and socializing within a country club atmosphere. The problem for me was this was a "retirement community." It was a community limited to residents who were fifty-five and older. These people wanted to make certain only quiet, gray and blue haired senior citizens lived in Leisureville. I'm not sure how my father slipped me into this neighborhood. Dad wasn't even fifty-five himself at the time. I was always told I looked older than I was, but at sixteen I don't think I could have passed for fifty-five. My parents asked all of the retired neighbors, who had nothing better to do, to keep an eye on me. Bernie and Margaret, who lived next door, were the nosiest people I ever meet and they were more than happy to keep an eye on me. They would actually look into my windows to see what I was up to. I quickly learned to keep my window blinds and curtains drawn all of the time. I was determined not to give these people free entertainment. My parents told them to call them if they thought they should know about anything. Well, my parents received numerous calls. My parents would then often call me asking who was over at my place and why there was a motorcycle in the front of my house. They knew more about what I did each day than when I lived at home.

After living on my own for a short time, I quickly learned to appreciate what a great deal I had when I slept under my parent's roof. My folk's home was a lot like living in a hotel. I had a meal plan consisting of three elegant and healthy meals a day and I had housekeeping services that included laundry services and linen changes. I was provided transportation and my parents paid all of the bills. Living on my own required me to learn how to cook and clean for myself. I was my own housekeeper now. I had to drive myself to school, pay the bills (with funds provided by mom and dad), shop for myself, go to the bank, and deal with all of the normal daily activities of life on my own, all while I still attended high school.

The first time I went to Publix, our local grocery store, I thought I had died and gone to heaven. I was like a child who discovered the hidden key to the candy cupboard. No one could tell me what to buy. I could skip the healthy products like oatmeal, wheat bread, fruits and vegetables and instead head straight for the junk food section. My food staples became Kellogg's Frosted Flakes also known as Tony the Tiger cereal, ice cream, nachos, pop corn, Coke, cookies, potato chips, chocolate and marshmallows. When I felt like eating something healthy, I would buy a complete pre-prepared dinner you could boil in the bag and just serve. My favorite was the boil-in-the-bag spaghetti or macaroni and cheese. All you needed to do was boil the bag. It was about as complicated a meal as I could muster.

No one ever showed me how to do laundry. I had no idea you needed to have a master's degree in chemistry before attempting to clean your clothes. I had one large pile of clothes I needed to wash, so I placed the one pile in one machine. I added a little bleach and the powered soap stuff and turned the machine on. When I opened the washing machine at the end of the washing cycle in order to place the clothes in the dryer, I noticed all of my clothes were now a bright pink color. No one told me colors needed separating, or that bleach was only for your white clothes. I had to buy all new underwear, socks and several shirts; but through trial and error, I finally learned how to my wash my clothes. I didn't own an iron and after the laundry fiasco I didn't want to attempt a new skill. I don't think I wore ironed clothes my entire senior year. It's a good thing the grunge look was in at the time.

Housekeeping was one of those things I dreaded to do. I would procrastinate doing any housekeeping until my neighbors threatened to call the health department. My dishes were washed only when I ran out of anything to eat on. The bathroom and shower needed cleaning annually, at least according to my maintenance schedule, and it was just in time for my one-year lease to be up. I had a vacuum cleaner, and I did actually vacuum a few times, but it never looked any different after I vacuumed than before. It was when my sister, Vered, visited me that she told me it was missing the rubber belt that goes around the brushes which turn and thereby clean the carpet. So I guess I never really vacuumed anything. Why bother to make your bed when all you were going to do was mess it up again in the evening. If you were brave enough to open a closet door in my apartment I would seriously recommend wearing a helmet as a precaution. Things were prone to fall on your head.

I was in real trouble when my car broke down. I had to somehow get it to the repair shop and get myself to school. I was able to ask a friend to help me out when that happened. The car I had at this time was a ten-year old Ford Monarch that was falling apart. My parents initially bought me a used 240-Z, a car made by the Japanese automaker Datsun, which later became Nissan. I wrecked the 240-Z after one-week of ownership by putting it in reverse and backing up at 40 miles per hour until I hit a pole that refused to get out of my way. As punishment for destroying the Z car, I received the Ford Monarch, a much bigger, slower, rusted out, old, burgundy-colored clunker; but I was happy they didn't take away my driving privileges.

When kids got thrown out of their house by their parents they would often end up at my door. Larry McGuinness, who was also a classmate of mine, offered to lease my sofa in the living room of my apartment. I didn't always like being by myself and I thought this would add some excitement as well as defray some of my costs. Larry made me look like Martha Stewart when it came to domestic chores. Larry would literally throw all of his trash and half eaten apple cores under his bed. But Larry was a lot of fun to have around. He was also on the speech team as well as on a host of other athletic teams. Larry would often get up at 4:00 AM to go jogging and would ask me if I wanted to join him. I always responded "No, and Hell No." I never understood why he was asked to leave his house. Maybe it was due to his refusal to do any chores. He never did any around the apartment. By the time we left this apartment I don't think it was habitable for humans anymore.

Pine Crest obviously did not know I was living on my own. I do not think they would have allowed this to continue if they ever found out. It was imperative I kept this a secret until I graduated, but it was going to be difficult once my closest friends discovered I had my own place.

Bill Kearney, a fiery, wily, redhead who was on the debate team with me, would often come by with his girlfriend Cara Catanzaro, a petite Italian sophomore. Cara had a large chest and actually nicknamed her boobs Charlie and Bob. Bill and Cara would come by my apartment and ask to use my shower. I initially thought they had some really good hygiene habits, but after they ripped my shower curtain off of its rod, I forbade them from using my bathroom again.

Then the pranks started. Someone would knock on the door and I would be hit by a Tsunami. A Tsunami is when someone fills a trashcan with water and leans it up against your door. They then knock on the door and run off. When you open the door, the trashcan weighing over a hundred pounds and filled with at least thirty gallons of water comes rushing into your home in this huge wave. A week after the Tsunami incident, Bill knocked on my door and sprayed a fire extinguisher into my apartment. The entire place was covered in a thick white powder that we were never able to clean up. Needless to say, when we I left the apartment I did not receive my security deposit back from the landlord.

To be fair to Bill, I also got him in a lot of trouble. I decided to set off firecrackers under Bill's window at his home. Unfortunately it was his parent's window, not Bill's, and his parent's thought they were being shot at. Shortly thereafter, Bill was asked to move out of the house. When Bill's parents finally calmed down after the firecracker incident, I decided to visit his home again. I could hear the conversation in the house as I hid outside near a bush by the front door.

Bill's mother asked his father, "Dudley are you working on the car?"

"No," he said.

"Then why is Bill's car sitting on concrete blocks, and why are his tires stacked up by the front door?"

Then I heard Bill exclaim "Oh Shit …"

I never understood why Bill's parents punished Bill every time I did something to him.

Throughout our senior year Wednesdays were euphemistically called "Wonder Wednesdays." Steve Holmes, Tim McGinty, Ed Wachtel, Andy Pond, Bill Kearney and I, as well as some other classmates, would get together at someone's home every Wednesday night. We would play poker, go out to the movies or just hang out together. Bill Kearney would always be the first one to fall asleep at our late night parties. It usually meant that Bill would wake up with a new haircut. We were bored and this was a wonderful way to amuse ourselves. Watching Bill's face as he woke up and realized his bright red hair was all over the sofa was enough to keep us laughing for at least another week. It was a good thing Bill's hair grew back quickly, so we could cut it again next week. Senior year was the time of my life, and as at it came to a close, I became really concerned that I would never have this much fun again.

34. A Higher Education

There was a Protestant horticulturist, an Irish Catholic pharmacist, and a German-Jewish banker ... this sounds like a preamble to some sort of joke, but these men were the founders of the university that I chose to attend and that chose to accept me, the University of Southern California.

The University was located in the heart of downtown Los Angeles. It was only a few short miles from South Central L.A, where the 1965 Watts riots erupted. The area around USC was a virtual no man's land. There were abandoned gas stations, vacant lots, and black-iron bars over the one-story bungalows where many of the African Americans, who were the dominant minority in this community, lived. Like most inner cities in America, it had plenty of poverty, frustration and hopelessness. But I grew up in New York near neighborhoods that were far worse, and as long as I stayed on campus I always felt safe.

The student population was about 30,000. The original school mascot was a feisty stray dog named George Tire Biter, but thankfully by the time I attended, it was Tommy Trojan. USC was an outstanding institution. It had the country's first filmmaking program, and it had a top-notch medical school and law school. More athletes were sent to the Olympic Games from USC than any other University. Unfortunately, I wasn't accepted into the film school, medical or law schools, nor was I heading to the Olympic Games. I was accepted into the business school.

My parents lived in Granada Hills about an hour's drive from USC, if there wasn't any traffic. The thing is in L.A. there is no such thing as no-traffic on the freeway. Part of my deal with my folks was if they let me stay in Florida my senior year in high school, I would attend a college near their home in California.

The home on Rushing Drive was a four-bedroom single story builder's model home. My father purchased it fully furnished. The only room with my mother's unique touch was the discotheque. It had a one-inch thick clear plexi-glass raised floor laid on top of psychedelic lights pulsating to the sound of the music. When you flipped on the light switch, the mirrored ball hanging from the ceiling would begin to spin and a hundred refracted light beams would twirl around the room.

Even though it was possible for me to live at home where I could disco my nights away, I chose to live in a University apartment. Some of the older dorms in University Park were built in the late 1800's or early 1900's. They had squeaky floors, long, dark, narrow hallways, tiny rooms with the typical slanted Venetian blinds, sagging beds, and broken dresser drawers. I got lucky and was assigned to a brand new apartment building that was only one block off the main campus.

I was given the suite number for my two-bedroom apartment and I was anxious to meet my three new roommates. As soon as I arrived in my new home, I set down my bags and introduced myself to the three guys who were already there. They shook my hand without seeming at all interested in me.

I sensed immediately something wasn't right. They were whispering amongst themselves. One of my roommates came up to me and with his eyes gazing down on the carpeting said, "I have a favor to ask of you."

I asked in a quiet tone of voice "What is it?"

"We want you to move," he said without looking up.

I explained tersely, "This is the apartment I was assigned to. Where exactly do you expect me to move to? Anyway, it usually takes a few hours to get to know me before you get decide you don't like me."

He looked up at me, with sorry written all over his face, and said, "No, it has nothing to do with you. The three of us went to high school together and we have a friend of who also went to the same high school. He was assigned to the fourth floor of this building. We were hoping you could switch places with him so we could share this apartment."

I thought about it for a moment. It was pretty evident I couldn't stay in this apartment; they would hate me if I stayed. I didn't know anybody anyhow. What difference would it make which floor I was on?

I made them wait a few minutes while I acted like I was still undecided. I bit my bottom lip and loosened my shirt collar. Finally I said in a light-hearted voice "It will cost you a case of Heineken," and I grabbed my bags and headed up to the fourth floor. Two hours after I settled into my new apartment, my former roommates from the second floor knocked on our door and delivered my moving out gift.

My new roommates on the fourth floor were a motley crew. Lee Klinghofer was a Jewish kid from New York and was in the School of Theater. Young was from Korea and majored in petroleum engineering. Lee and Young shared one of the two bedrooms. Jeff Oster was a six foot nine inch giant who shared my room. He was a California native studying business. In a way it felt like I was back in the New York melting pot. We were two Jews, an Asian and a Giant living under one roof.

Young mainly kept to himself and studied in his room with the door closed. The only time we knew he was in the apartment was when we could smell this pungent odor wafting through our living room. It smelled like someone left a rotting carcass in our home. Young was eating kimchi. This was a Korean delicacy made of a vegetable called baechu, or Chinese cabbage, and was fermented like pickles. It was highly seasoned with garlic, vinegar, green onions, soy sauce, and bean paste. Young used to offer us some kimchi, but none of us would even consider trying it. He used to say in his thick Korean accent, "It's good for you, the rrractic (lactic) acid produced in the fermentation process suppresses the growth of any harmful bacteria in the intestines, and the cabbage is high in fiber and prevents constipation." "The garlic," he said proudly, "prevents intestinal cancer." We all believed him. We knew no living organism would dare to grow in this concoction. But Young was destroying our social lives. No one dared visit us when the apartment smelled like fermented cabbage and garlic. Finally, we forbade him from eating kimchi. I guess he didn't appreciate being denied his traditional food. He moved out after the first semester of school was over.

Lee was a typical New Yorker; he had the requisite accent and high-energy. He was an animated kid with bushy black hair, a big nose and freckles. When he wasn't walking around the apartment talking to himself while he was memorized his lines, he would practice his song and dance numbers in the only room that was not carpeted, our bathroom. The bathroom had a linoleum floor covering where he could tap-dance. Lee's classmates would often come by and would head straight into our bathroom and start dancing. Ally Sheady, who went on to star in *The Breakfast Club* and *Short Circuit,* as well as actor, director and producer Forest Whitaker, who starred in *Platoon,* were some of the drama majors who used our bathroom as their stage. Unfortunately Lee was not among the lucky ones. I never heard from him again after college.

Jeff could not walk into our apartment without ducking his head under the doors. When he went to sleep his feet would hang over the end of his bed. He had to take a chair and set it at the bottom of his bed as an extension so his feet didn't dangle down. Buying clothes was a nightmare for him. If he was lucky enough to find something that fit, he had to pay a substantial premium for it. I don't know how many times I saw him clutching his knees as he tried to scrunch into a seat. Airline seats didn't offer him enough leg room and compact cars didn't offer him enough headroom. When he rode with me in my Toyota Celica, we had to open the sunroof so he could fit in the car. He must have felt like circus clown with his head sticking out above my miniature Celica.

I lost count of how many times people would come up to him and say "Damn, how tall are you? Do you play basketball?" He'd then give his standard reply, "6' 9, and I did play in high school, but I injured by knees and back, so I don't play anymore." Jeff would always tell me how much his neck and back hurt at the end of a typical day of looking down at everyone.

Having a roommate who was vertically gifted had its advantages. He could easily intimidate people. If we went out to a busy bar or restaurant, all we had to do was stand next to a table and people would clear out quickly. When I was with Jeff, no one would mess with me. I could go up to people and tell them, "You're a real jerk and by the way this is my roommate." Anytime I lost him in a crowd, all I had to do was look up. At the market I could point to the top shelf and say, "Jeff can you get that?" Women would ask him, "Are all of your body parts as gigantic as you are?" Jeff's would smile slyly and then respond "If you are really interested, I am willing to let you find out." But the truth was Jeff had a hard time finding girls tall enough to date. When we first became roommates, I was dumb enough to split food costs with him. It didn't take me long to figure out he was eating three times as much as I was. We decided we would each get our own shelf in the fridge and keep our food separate from that point on.

After Young left our apartment we got another roommate who was in the USC School of Music. Ron played a long dark-colored woodwind instrument with silver metal keys called the oboe. It was similar to a clarinet, but unlike a clarinet it didn't have a mouthpiece; it had two reeds tied together. These double reeds fit into a tube at the top of the instrument and vibrated when air was forced between the reeds, which were made of cane. You had to be a little strange in 1979 to want to play only classical music. Out of all of the possible instruments one could play, he chose the oboe. Ron sat ramrod straight in the living room and did his breathing exercises. I thought this guy was purposefully trying to hyperventilate. He would lecture us on proper breathing techniques and posture. "Breath deeply from the diaphragm," he would say. I didn't know where the diaphragm was, or what it did, and I didn't care to. The nut would walk around the apartment breathing deeply like he was a tube of toothpaste being squeezed at the bottom. Then his hour-long warm up exercises would begin. Ron would do an hour of scales over and over again. He would start with high G and go down to B flat and do all of the major and minor scales. The oboe was a high-pitched instrument and he didn't have his fingering techniques down yet. The sound was frightening. Just when you were sure you couldn't take it anymore and you were going to have to kill yourself, he would start his metronome. He set it at the fastest speed he could. The high pitched squeal of the oboe combined with the tick tock sound of the metronome made me long for the smell of kim-chi.

35. Penis Called

I entered my apartment at the end of what was a tough day of classes and noticed a large sheet of lined paper by the phone. It was a hand written note from Jeff addressed to me in large bold black letters. The note read, "Penis called for you and would like you to call him back." I knew right then and there I was going to be the laughing-stock of my entire apartment building. Penis was my sister Vered's new boyfriend, but his name was Pinchas, not Penis. I'm certain with his heavy Israeli accent it sounded like he said my name is Penis. To make matters worse, Pinchas preferred to be called Pini for short, which to most Americans sounds like many penises. Pini was of all things, a hairdresser. I told my sister "You know most hair dressers who are male are not straight … right?" She assured me he was straight.

I asked her "Why on earth would a male want to be a hairdresser? What possible satisfaction could he get? Can't you date normal people with normal names?

As soon as I met Pini he offered to give me a haircut, and I quickly got the answers to my questions. He became a hairdresser because of the sheer power that comes with the job. He gets to place you in his hairdresser hot seat. Next, he puts a cape around you covering your arms like a straight jacket. When you are armless and helpless, he asks you with a slight smirk on his face and a raised eyebrow, "How would you like to have your hair done?" You know by the way he is looking at you, he is going give you the haircut he wants, regardless of what you want. Then he takes these sharp tools to your head and slices your hair with scissors. If you're not nice to him, in just a few seconds he can have you sobbing in front of his mirror desperately clutching what's left of your hair. Anyone who has ever had a bad experience with his hairdresser can tell you that getting a trim and a blow dry from the wrong man or women can be a very traumatic event. Off course hair usually grows back, but hair is a key component of our self-esteem, and having a bad cut can seriously damage it.

Pinchas was a professional. He was a hair alchemist who had a whole year of training and a certificate to prove it. He could augment, braid, comb, curl, color, perm, sculpt, tease and twist with the best of them. Curling irons, hairspray, pins, rollers, brushes, combs, clippers and scissors in his hands were like scalpels in a surgeon's.

Even though he didn't have a degree in psychology, Pini was a therapist who could delve deep into his customers' psyches while they were being shampooed. Like most hairdressers he was a good conversationalist with a special talent for listening. Since Hebrew was his first language, it was possible he never understood what his American customers were saying, but acting like you were listening was what was important with his job.

Pini ran the salon with his partner David Babyoff. When I first meet both of them I asked my sister, "Are you sure these two aren't a couple?"

She looked puzzled and asked said, "A couple of what?"

"You know, a couple-couple," I said, winking at her.

She responded, "No way, as a matter of fact, they are related to each other through the marriages of their siblings, and David was married once before and has children from his previous marriage."

I then asked her with a straight face, "Do you know what the probability is of having two straight males in the same hair salon? Slim, very slim," I said.

When Pini got serious about Vered, Edna decided she wasn't going to be left behind and started to date David. Edna was already divorced from a man she claimed was too weird for our family (if you can believe that). She was looking to start over and David, who was at least twenty years older than Edna, was interested. Free hairstyling for life was just too good of a deal for Edna to pass up. Vered and Pini were secretly married in Israel. They didn't invite me to the wedding or even tell me until long after they were already married. The reason had something to do with Pini already being married to someone else. In order to get his green card and work in the U.S. as a legal resident, he married an American on paper only. He couldn't get divorced for a number of years after he got his green card even though he was now really marrying an American citizen. He had to wait to file for divorce in the U.S. I guess they didn't invite me because they were afraid I would tell someone. Who would I ever tell? Since Vered had taken the plunge, Edna wasn't going to be far behind. Edna married David shortly after Vered's marriage. We were now one big happy convoluted family, but at least it entitled me to free haircuts.

36. Lessons from Abroad

Studying abroad sounded intriguing. USC offered programs in France, Italy, England and Spain. Since I did not speak French or Italian and England was too expensive, Spain was my only real choice. I took Spanish in high school and although I was far from fluent I could at least communicate.

When you travel to a new country everything is exhilarating and exciting. The sights, sounds and tastes are all a new adventure. I would get to learn about the culture, improve my language skills, and take USC courses taught by USC approved professors. Our classes were held in the USC Madrid Center in a beautiful building that was the former embassy for the United States. It was located in an upscale section of Madrid near several cultural institutions and other foreign embassies. This was a once-in-a-lifetime opportunity. I would get to travel throughout Europe, North Africa and the Middle East. In just a matter of hours you could be in Paris, London, Barcelona, Rome, Tangier, or wherever your heart and your Eurail Train Pass could take you.

Upon our arrival in Madrid we were set up in a hotel near the school where we went through our orientation. Madrid was a high-energy, fast-moving, commercialized city and we couldn't wait to start exploring it. We had the choice of staying with local families willing to host us, or of finding and renting an apartment on our own.

Rick Simmons, Cindy Shepard, Leah Smith and I were in the minority of students who chose to live in our own apartment. Having our own place allowed us to be as independent and adventurous as we wanted. The four of us decided we would share a two-bedroom furnished apartment that was on a list of recommended places provided to us by the school. It was in a neighborhood adjacent to USC's Madrid Center. The girls shared one bedroom while Rick and I shared the other. The interesting thing about the apartment was it had no phone, and cell phones did not exist yet. The only way to call home was to go to the main telephone company offices near the Cibeles Fountain and pay for a call to the U.S. Then you had to wait for the operator to tell you she had a line and direct you to one of a number of phone booths. Since calls to the States were difficult, time-consuming and costly, I did not make many during my semester in Madrid.

We didn't have a car in Madrid, but that wasn't a problem. The public transportation in Spain and the rest of Europe was amazing, especially when compared to California's. There wasn't much room for cars on the roads in Madrid and gas was very expensive anyway. A bus, subway or the main rail lines could take you wherever you wanted to go. The only problem with the subways was how common pick-pocketing was, especially of tourists and foreigners. I felt someone trying to pull my wallet out of my back pant pocket at a train station, luckily my hand swung back in time to stop my wallet from disappearing. You needed to be aware of your belongings and surroundings when you traveled.

Before I arrived in Madrid I packed like my mother. I took more suitcases than any of the girls did in this program. When we arrived in Madrid it was cool at night. You needed a winter coat, hat and gloves, but by the time our semester was over the temperature was in the nineties. I had to have every contingency covered. I also had a lot of camera gear, a still 35mm camera, numerous different lenses, an 8mm-movie camera and tripods. I talked Rick Simmons into carrying all of my camera gear wherever we went. I told him I would take pictures of him so he would have something to remember this trip by.

Rick was also a business major. We both scheduled all of our classes to start on Monday and end on Thursday. It meant we had three-day weekends every weekend. I took classes in philosophy, international relations, Spanish, international business and business communications. It obviously depended on the professor, but most classes started late; the teacher's were very laid back, and the classes were typically small. All of my classes with the exception of Spanish were taught in English. Our grades depended on one or two quizzes, a final exam, an assignment or two, plus a research paper in a few of the classes. Studying philosophy and international relations with a Spaniard for a professor gave me the opportunity to see the world through someone else's eyes. Many of the Spaniards who were our age thought of Americans as uncultured, overworked, and cold. Rick and I showed the "Nards", which is what we called them for short, that we were not overworked, we were as lazy as they were, and we were clearly warm blooded, and after visiting fifty museums, we were as cultured as any European.

Madrid was a city full of life, which wasn't limited to the party crowd that appeared after dark. During the day the streets were full of people. Walking was the most common form of transportation. Coffeehouses had tables outside where you could hear the music of the street musicians mixed with the conversations of the locals. You could sit, read, talk or simply watch the world go by.

There was never a vacant park bench. I guess young amorous Spaniards lived at home and had nowhere else to go. Public displays of affection on park benches were a very common sight.

Prior to living in Spain, the last time I took a nap was in kinder-garten. In Madrid naps were not just for kids. From two to five in the afternoon the city shut down, kids were let out of school, adults got off work, and stores closed. Families went home and enjoyed a large meal together and took a nap.

Spain's crazy nightlife and parties were part of its culture. The dinner hour started at about 10:00 PM when fried foods and wine was served. Tapas bars served snack-sized portions of chorizo, tomatoes, cheese, meats, and cervesas or beers. The tapas bars were packed until 2:00 AM. Then the hoards of people were off to the discotheques. The naps in the afternoon became a necessity because it was the only time the Nards got to sleep. Spaniards enjoy life more then we do. They "work to live, not live to work."

If you purchased a Eurail Pass in the U.S. before you left, which we all did, you could use all of the main train systems throughout Europe without having to buy additional tickets. All we had to do to get away was pack a toothbrush and a few clothes, and head to the train station. You could fall asleep in one country and wake up in a different one. Rick Simmons and I would grab a "Let's Go Europe" guidebook and head for a new country, attraction, festival, concert or city each weekend.

On one of our first weekends Rick and I decided to visit Granada. It is a city located next to the Sierra Nevada Mountains in Andalusia in the south of Spain. Granada is also only 70 km from the coast. It was a place you could ski in the mountains in the morning and sunbathe on the beach in the late afternoon. . Granada's cobblestoned streets with whitewashed houses and Moorish architecture had a strong Arabic feeling. Arabic sultans and Caliphs once ruled Granada. The Arabic Empire stretched right up to the north of Spain until the Catholic monarchs Isabel and Ferdinand forced the Muslims and Jews to leave the country, convert to Christianity or face execution.

Rick and I had just finished a day of skiing and were walking around the Albaicin, which is the old Arabic quarter located on the hill opposite the Alhambra, the castle of the Sultans who ruled this province, when all of a sudden we heard someone yell "Gil, Gil, Gil." I turned around and saw Kevin Hyman walking down the same street. Kevin was a USC student from California, who I had met two days prior to leaving for Spain. He told me he was taking a year off of school and was going to be in Europe when I was there. He had asked if he could meet up with me, but I wasn't expecting him now, and definitely not in Granada.

I said "Kevin what a coincidence to meet you in Granada."

He replied, "It's no coincidence, I came here looking for you."

I raised my eyebrow in surprise and said, "What do you mean you came here looking for me? How did you know I was in Granada?"

"I went to the USC Madrid Center and asked the administrator if he knew where you were. He said he thought you had gone to Granada for the weekend," he said nonchalantly.

"Granada is a city of over a quarter of a million people; how did you know where I was going to be?" I said, still baffled.

Kevin said, "It didn't matter if I found you; I heard Granada was a great college town and thought it would be fun even if I didn't meet up with you."

After our Granada weekend Kevin came back with Rick and me and stayed in our apartment for a while. He then went off on his own through the rest of Europe, but we agreed to get together back in California when our semester ended.

After several tame weekend trips around Madrid we decided to visit a country that was more exotic, Morocco. There are only nine choppy ocean miles separating Algeciras in Southern Spain from Tangier in North Africa. A one-hour ferry ride past the Rock of Gibraltar and you were very far from Europe, in a land totally unfamiliar. As we disembarked the ferry, Tangiers awaited us. I was dying to tell someone, anyone, to … "Take me to the Kasbah."

Tangiers was pure anarchy. This port city was the Tijuana of Morocco and the capital of crime. The first thing Rick and I noticed when we went through customs was a wall full of pictures of missing children. We were told when the sun sets the city is unsafe. I was just as concerned when the sun was straight overhead as I was after dark. The police, local authorities and the mafia were all working together. The beach town was filthy, kids begged for money on every corner, there was no running water in the old town, pickpockets were everywhere, and "Official Guides" tried to scam you as soon as you disembarked from the ferry.

After pushing away a very aggressive guide who gripped my forearm tightly and tried to strong-arm me into hiring him, I told Rick we should get the hell out as soon as possible. We walked to a nearby café and sat down on a sidewalk full of diesel clouds from the passing cars and buses. We ordered some mint tea. As soon as we sat down, a swarthy Moroccan named Ahmed decided to join us.

"Where are you from? What's your name? Where are you staying? He unabashedly asked. He then said, "Do you like to smoke hashish?"

Rick and I looked at each other in disbelief. We finished our tea as soon as possible and left without talking to Ahmed. We ran down the street through the gate to the Medina near the Great Mosque and walked until it connected directly to the beach. The streets were all very narrow and the anonymous facades of the buildings all looked alike. We were quickly getting lost in a very dangerous place. The Medina had the worst reputation in Tangier. This was the place where drug deals were made, where human smuggling occurred and prostitution was rampant. The ferry back to Spain was not available until the next morning and we were concerned about making it through the night.

As we walked through the market our senses were assaulted. The scent of sulphur hung in the air. The smell of fish and spices, shit and urine permeated the place. Hoards of humanity were walking through the narrow and winding streets. A cacophony of voices from tourists and locals haggling over the prices in French, English, Spanish and Arabic rang in our ears. Flies were attacking us and where-ever you looked sweaty shopkeepers were shaking their index fingers wildly at their customers. It was an alien environment in a medieval world unlike anywhere else I had ever been. It was sensory overload.

In the market, Rick and I over heard a husband and wife who appeared to be American and spoke both Arabic and English. We interrupted their conversation and asked them for help. They were on a Peace Corp mission in Rabat, the capital of Morocco, and they were spending the day in Tangier. We asked them where they were staying and told them we were concerned for our safety. They lead us back to their hotel where we checked in and had a nice dinner with them. Robert and Sally convinced us that the rest of Morocco was not like Tangier, and it was well worth going with them to Rabat, just North of Casablanca, to get a taste of the real Morocco. Since they spoke the language and appeared to be comfortable in this environment we felt like we were in less danger. The next morning we decided to join our new friends from the Peace Corp. and took the train to Rabat. The trains in Morocco do not run on any real schedule. When you ask what time the train is supposed to arrive or depart they give you the time and then add an Inshaallah, which means G-d willing. The train will arrive 10:00 o'clock, G-d willing, and if the train arrives at 11:30 instead, well then G-d just didn't will it to be. As we rode through the countryside by train we saw a large camel caravan traversing the desert plains. This for the first time evoked images of the Arabian thousand and one nights I had expected.

Rabat is known as the "Royal City" because it is the seat of the Royal Family. This white and clean city faces the Atlantic Ocean and is situated on the estuary of a river. Unlike Tangier, Rabat was home to bewitching ornate palaces, parks, mosques and monuments. Near the main entrance to one of the palaces we saw a pair of color guards on white horses dressed in flame red tunics and trousers, bright green caps and polished black boots. The people here were far more gracious than in Tangier. Rick and I were glad we spent the extra time and got to see more than just the port city we disembarked from on the ferry. When we got back to Tangier from Rabat we headed straight for the ferry back to Spain.

Rick and I were both very relieved to have made it back safely.

By the time the semester ended Rick had carried my ninety pounds of camera equipment throughout Europe and North Africa. When he discovered I had taken only a handful of pictures of him, he was really ready to kill me.

37. A Higher Calling

While I was trotting around Europe, Lily was living alone with our parents in Granada Hills, California. While I was finding myself in Europe, Lily had to search for herself closer to home.

Even though I was told by my mother I was an ugly child and kids at school taunted me with "You're ugly and your mother dresses you funny," those hurtful words didn't have a lasting impact on me. I was constantly receiving positive reinforcement in other areas of my life and I felt good about myself. Unfortunately for my little sister, shallow thoughtless words did have a lasting and deeper impact on her.

"Life and Death are in the tongue, words can kill"- proverbs 18:1

Mom would tell Lily mockingly "You're fat; you have thick thighs, large hips, a round face and a big nose. If you don't lose weight, no one will want you. You'll never be a wife or a mother unless you do something with yourself."

The pressure to be thin in our society is everywhere. Underweight models and actresses, clothes designed for only thin figures, the images of slim women are inescapable. According to the Journal of the American Dietetic Association, one out of eight teen girls engage in "chronic dieting and thirty percent in binge eating."

Adults generally know charm is deceptive and beauty is fleeting, but teenagers are too immature to have learned those lessons yet. Lily became consumed by her body. She placed more importance on her body than her heart. Dissatisfaction with the body often stems from a desire to be loved and accepted and Lily wasn't getting much of either.

She would starve herself for as many days as she could and when she couldn't take the hunger anymore she would eat in an uncontrollable fit. She grew obsessed with her eating habits and her weight fluctuated wildly. Her episodes of binge eating were followed by inappropriate purging or vomiting. This wasn't a response to hunger. It was a response to depression, stress, self-esteem issues and self-loathing.

Like most people who do battle with their bodies, she kept it a secret from everyone. But the telltale signs were there. Lily brushed her teeth constantly and she would often excuse herself to go to the bathroom after every meal. Her hair started to thin and her eyes looked pained and lack luster. Weight obsessions can cause you to do harmful and destructive things.

Lily eventually married Hanan Eden. I don't know what it is with my sisters marrying people who have names no one can pronounce, but Lily decided to do it. She was under a lot of pressure to get married and married the first Mercedes Benz she could find.

I never understood how someone could find a soul mate when they haven't yet located their own soul. I told Hanan he should wait to get married. "What's the rush," I said. "Lily isn't ready," I told him bluntly. But they wouldn't listen and they were married and divorced within a few years. Lily had a baby with Hanan they named Eve. She was named after my grandmother Ahuva. My sister raised her until she was three years old, and then she lost her to Hanan in a terrible custody fight. Lily was going to make Aliyah to Israel with her new husband, and the courts would not allow her to take her child out of the United States.

It took Lily a long time to learn that G-d made her as he intended her to be. Lily married her second husband, who was newly orthodox, and they moved to Jerusalem where she found strength in religion. When I talk to my sister these days, she says she prays a lot.

I asked her, "Does He answer you? Do you hear voices?"

Her reply was, "Sometimes he answers right away, sometimes it takes more time, and sometimes the answer is no; and no, I don't hear voices, but I do feel He looks out for me."

Lily showed our mother a thing or two; she was not only able to find a husband; she was able to find two, and as far as being a mother was concerned, she would outdo all of us. She has had a total of nine kids. If anyone had told me one day my little sister would be the mother of nine kids I would have laughed in their face and recommended a good psychiatrist. In addition to Eve, she had Moriah, Shiriah, Taliah, Josh, Matt, Shani, Shemaiah and Ataria, aka Tara. The bible says, "Nothing is to interfere with the highest calling a person can have, which is raising children." No one could argue with the fact Lily clearly answered that call.

38. Life on the Beach

When we returned to California from Madrid, Kevin Hyman made Rick Simmons and me an offer we couldn't refuse. His parents had a three-bedroom condo right on Santa Monica Beach. It was sandwiched in between Baron Hilton's seaside mansion and the most exclusive beach club in California, The Jonathan Club. We could live with Kevin and another friend, Brian Boudreau, for the monthly rental rate of zero. Kevin's parents let us have it for free.

We were college students living in a million-dollar beachfront home, back when a million dollars was still considered a lot of money. Although the condo was luxurious, we were still college students who couldn't afford any real furniture for the place. Our place was "Retro" before anyone knew what "Retro" was. The refrigerator we purchased was manufactured around 1950, and apparently hadn't been defrosted since then. The freezer compartment was a frozen solid block of ice. Instead of defrosting it, we chipped out just enough room to slide in a bottle of Russian Stolichnaya vodka. During the entire year we lived in Santa Monica, it was the only thing that went into our freezer. Other than some orange juice the fridge rarely had any food in it. The four of us would always go out for meals. Brian's father had a conference room table, which he let us use as our dining room table, and we each brought our beds from home. We purchased a lime green vinyl sofa and a large green bean bag for the living room. I have no idea how or why lime green became our dominant furniture color; it didn't match anything else in the condo. Apparently, no one else wanted it.

Our condo epitomized beach life in Southern California. We could literally step out of our back door and ride a wave or wade in one. We could hear the cry of seagulls and smell the sea-salted air or just sit there and people-watch. The view from the second story balcony was of a clear three-and-a-half mile stretch of beach, the rocky cliffs across the street and the beach volleyball courts.

Santa Monica was a tranquil seaside city with a diverse population. The desperately poor walked alongside the incredibly affluent. Senior citizens lived next to young yuppies and college students. Beach Babes strolled along the shore next to weathered fisherman sitting on their five-gallon buckets holding their rods. It was a city in motion. The streets were lined with unique shops, elegant dining, street performers and musicians. Santa Monica Boulevard, better known as "Route 66," ended its winding national run right in front of our door.

This city was the epicenter for fitness. It was the birthplace of beach volleyball and was the original Muscle Beach. Woven throughout the town were bike paths, roller-blading lanes, and jogging trails. But all of this athleticism never rubbed off on me. I never had the urge to do more than wade in the water or walk on the beach. Just watching everyone running, biking, blading, jumping and sweating taxed me.

My three roommates were all great athletes. Rick Simmons was in tip-top shape thanks to the weight-lifting opportunities I provided him in Europe lugging my camera equipment around. Brian Boudreau looked and dressed like a model for GQ, always wearing Armani, and Kevin Hyman came from a long line of high school athletic coaches and took every sport very seriously. My roommates were buff, sun-baked, and preppy California beach boys. I was the brainy, near-sighted, former New Yorker who never quite fit in this "Baywatch" scene.

I have a theory about groups of friends who seem to have at least one member who isn't as good-looking as everyone else. The reason, at least according to my theory, is keeping this person around makes the other members look even better than they would normally. It acts as an even greater Babe magnet. Every group has at least one person who fills this role. If someone isn't sure who that person is in their group, he needs to have a good look in the mirror.

When the four of us went out on dates together, I was doomed to get the girl who was blind, or had one leg shorter than the other, or had Tourette's syndrome. It wasn't a pretty sight when my dates started flailing their arms and making weird gasping sounds. I knew that if I was ever going to find a "normal girl" I would have to find her on my own, and keep her away from my roommates.

If looks weren't enough to give Kevin and Brian an edge with the ladies, they also had all of the toys of stereotypically rich U.S.C. (University of Spoiled Children) students. Brian drove a new Mercedes Benz, and Kevin's father had a yacht in Marina del Rey.

The Marina was only a fifteen-minute drive from our condo. It was the largest man-made pleasure craft harbor in the world and was ringed by upscale hotels and restaurants. The scene was of endless yachts moored and floating on mild waters in an atmosphere of total serenity. We were hedonists sipping cocktails and nibbling appetizers and relaxing to the point of slothfulness. I couldn't wait for the chance to invite a "normal girl" to share this with me.

39. A Normal Girl

It's difficult to predict what might come of the smallest of our daily actions. A chance meeting in a USC library was about to change everything. I'm always astounded by how simply things begin. I was looking for a reference book for an assignment in my accounting class. I looked everywhere but the book was missing, so I went up to the reference desk and asked the librarian for help. At the front desk, I noticed a cute girl who wasn't blind, appeared to have two legs of the same length, and did not spontaneously begin to scream profanities at me. Her name was Barbara. Professor Deanna Daniels gave our entire accounting class an extra credit project in which we had to research a specific publicly held company. Barbara had the same accounting class, although hers was during a different period than mine, and she needed the same reference book. Library reference books were not supposed to be checked out, but the librarian's attempt to locate the book proved to be futile. After the librarian came back to tell Barbara and me she could not find the book, I decided to ask Barbara out to lunch.

I liked the idea of a quick lunch for our first date. The worst is when you plan an entire evening and it isn't working out. It's like a hostage situation where you are being held against your will, and you can't escape. Then at the end of the evening, you get to pay a ransom to the restaurant. Lunch, on the other hand, is great. You're in, you're out, and nobody gets hurt. All humans dread first dates. They are excruciatingly awkward. They produce more anxiety and pressure than job interviews. There is always the possibility for heart-wrenching rejection or getting brushed off like a gnat. But luckily Barbara said, "Yes." We walked across the street to Burger King for what would be our first and only fast food meal together. The goal of any first date is to break the ice, to get to know each other, and create an atmosphere that sparks a friendship and hopefully ignites a wild romance. Although, I'm not sure Barbara ever thought of this as our first date. It was more of a meeting between classmates.

"So what's an engineering major doing in an accounting class" I asked, puzzled.

She responded, "It's a requirement for engineers to take a few business classes, and accounting is one of the required classes."

"So what kinds of things do you like to do in your spare time?" I inquired.

"Unfortunately, I have very little spare time. I work for Northrop when I'm not in class," she said.

"How can you work full time and go to USC full time?" I asked amazed.

"Northrop offered me full tuition reimbursement. It was the only way I could pay for USC," she said nonchalantly.

I was really impressed, but I tried not to show it. The worst thing I could do on our first date was to fawn over her. Girls enjoy getting attention almost as much as they savor shooting down the men who give it to them. It's counter-intuitive, but if you're interested in someone, you shouldn't pay too much attention to them. Barbara was beautiful. But beauty in Southern California was common. It's something one was either born with, or if you went to USC, you could pay for. To me what counted was that she was making something of herself. I was trying to come across as someone who was confident, nice, and not too aggressive or too timid. It must have worked, because when we finished our Whoppers, fries and Cokes, she gave me her phone number.

40. Dating Games

I knew every decision I was about to make could affect whether or not we developed a relationship. So the strategies I employed rivaled any chess match I played. I planned every move in anticipation of my opponent's move. But this opponent was an extraterrestrial. All women are; I'm certain of it. They have the ability to hear multiple conversations simultaneously over great distances. Just watch them in a restaurant; they can tell you what everyone is saying across the entire room. They also have other supernatural powers, like enhanced peripheral vision. Men stare at things like a starving dog does when he sees a piece of meat, but women have the ability to see 360 degrees without even turning their heads. They know if you are staring at them, even if it looks like they are looking at the floor. I knew I had to prepare for this encounter.

I thought to myself, "Where do I take her on our second date?"

"It needs to be better than Burger King."

"What do I say to her?"

If I said something like, "You look nice," she might start thinking, "What does he mean ... nice? Am I too fat in this outfit? Does he really mean I look nice, or is he just saying that?"

"Do I tell her I like her shoes? I don't know anything about shoes, and I could care less about shoes. I'm certain she will be able to tell I'm being disingenuous. I have to give this matter some thought."

I had to also plan spontaneity into the evening. If things went well, I needed to be prepared to say, "I have an idea, let's go here," and I would spontaneously have a great second place to take her to. If the date was not going well, I needed to be able to cut the evening short.

It was Friday night. I showered, splashed on some cologne, brushed my teeth and hair, and reminded myself to eat with my mouth closed. I then drove to Barbara's dorm in my Toyota Celica.

I chose to take her to the Bicycle Shop Café on Wilshire Boulevard in West Los Angeles. It was strategically located less than ten miles from Santa Monica Beach. The Café combined the best in atmosphere and French California cuisine. It had every imaginable type of bike from antique to modern hanging from the walls and ceiling. The bikes would give us something to talk about. The food was great, the service was first class, and every Friday night they had live Jazz music. I had just made my first move.

Sometimes we pretend to be someone else for these dates. It's almost an out-of-body experience. We set up fictitious personalities, act smarter, dress more fashionably, and practice our best lines. I could tell Barb was nervous and was trying to impress me. She was using a vocabulary of six and seven syllable words. Barb was either trying to see if I had a comparable vocabulary to hers, or she was trying to impress me with her superior intellect. In either case, I was sick of the plastic personalities, the thin veneers and sappy smiles of the girls I recently dated, so I had very little patience for this game. I thought this night was going to end early.

I finally turned to Barb and said, "Are you always so full of it?"

She smiled and seemed to instantaneously drop the façade she was displaying for my benefit. It seems the more you push woman away, the more they are attracted to you. The fact I had the confidence to tell her she was full of it, impressed her more than anything else I had said or done all evening. Go figure. After an evening of great food and music, I suggested we take a walk on the beach in Santa Monica and have a nightcap at my place.

41. The Way to Her Heart

I received a call from Barbara on a Sunday morning asking me if I had a camera, and if I did, could I take a few black and white pictures of her. I told her I would be happy to take pictures of her, but I asked her what she needed them for. She told me she was applying for a scholarship offered by the Rotary Club to an abroad program at the University of Leeds in England. The application required a head shot of her in black and white. It was supposed to be mailed no later than Monday morning and she didn't realize they needed a picture. I was stunned. The thought of her going off to Europe never to be seen again depressed me. Maybe if I took terrible pictures of her she would be rejected, I thought. But after some consideration, I decided not to sabotage her chances. Who was I to deny her this opportunity? She knew I had a wonderful experience in Spain. I took her pictures and developed them for her in the USC film school lab and gave them to her the same day.

I decided I should still try to convince her to stay and began a protracted debate about why going to England was a bad idea. "You know you're going to be in a totally alien environment? They don't speak American out there." I said emphatically. "I'm sure I'll get by," she retorted. "I'm not even certain they will accept me. Let's not worry about what happens until I get the University's response."

"Are you kidding?" I said astonished. "You graduated at the top of your high school class, you received a USC Presidential Scholarship, you basically work as a rocket scientist at Northrop, and you are one of a very small group of women in engineering. If they don't accept you, who do you think they are going to accept?"

"I don't know, but let's wait and see," she added.

"Leeds is in Northeast England. It's always cold, dark, dank and it rains all of the time," I said.

"I'm from Oregon, I'm used to the rain." She responded.

"True," I conceded, "but the only thing Leeds is known for is the Corn Exchange and The Royal Armories Museum. I didn't know you were into corn and arms," I said with a smirk on my face.

"I'm sure there will be more to do than visit the Exchange and the Armory," she said.

"Yes, like watching a game of cricket. The British refer to it as a gentlemanly game played at a leisurely pace. I would rather listen to a golf game on the radio than be subjected to cricket," I said mockingly. "Their food is horrible. They eat black pudding for breakfast. It looks like a black sausage, but it's made of dried pigs blood and fat. Then they eat haggis for dinner. Haggis is made of a sheep's stomach bag, stuffed with dry oatmeal, lamb's liver, chopped mutton suet, and minced onion," I said, looking at her for a reaction. It was the first time she looked concerned. I was getting to her.

Barbara was becoming a food connoisseur with all of my wining and dining. I quickly learned she never forgot a meal. When it came to food, Barbara had T.T.R. or *Total Taste Recall*. She was someone with a photographic memory on her tongue. When Barb talked about a food she would inhale deeply during the discussion as if she could smell and taste the meal we were talking about. Once her taste buds were stimulated the flavor and smell was permanently imprinted on her brain. When she ate freshly baked crusty Italian bread rubbed with a little garlic and drizzled with olive oil, her face would contort with ecstasy and her eyes would roll to the back of her head. I discovered her weakness, her Achilles heel. It was food.

My strategy would be deceptively simple. I would sway her to stay by combining romantic and decadent meals with exotic ones.

Our romantic meals were at the Mustache Café on Melrose Avenue in Los Angeles. The ambience of a candle-lit dinner under the stars, in the garden patio where the trees were covered in small white twinkling lights, set the mood. The waitresses were beautiful and the diverse clientele consisted of a young Hollywood, preppy crowd. We started with the impressive wine selection and worked our way up to the warm artichoke dip appetizer. Finally we ordered our crepe dinners at the same time as our desserts. It took forty-five minutes for them to prepare the individually baked chocolate soufflés. They were delivered piping hot with vanilla bean ice cream and freshly whipped cream on top.

The exotic dinners consisted of a traditional Moroccan feast in a re-created fifteenth-century palace called Dar Maghreb. It was located on Sunset Boulevard. The exterior was a chalk-white building with understated brass Arabic lettering on it. There were massive hand-hammered brass doors at the entrance, in an archway reminiscent of a Moorish castle, like the Alhambra in Spain. When we entered, we were ushered into a beautifully decorated room of rich blues and gold past a splashing fountain with walls decorated in elaborate tile. The seating was on pillows on the floor. The waiter then performed the traditional hand-washing ceremony by bringing a large brass bowl and pouring a tall stream of water over our hands from a brass pot as he stood four feet above us.

Dinner began with harira, a traditional Moroccan lentil soup. Then they brought out the salades marocaines, which were cooked and marinated vegetable salads. The b'stilla was next. It was a flaky pastry shell stuffed with chicken, almonds, eggs and spices, baked with butter and sprinkled with powdered sugar and cinnamon. I could see Barb was armed with a hearty appetite as she sank her teeth into each course using her bare hands. The main course was tagine de poulet aux citrons. Its ingredients consisted of chicken with pickled lemon rinds and olives on a bed of couscous, or wheat semolina. A Moroccan dessert of dried and fresh fruit, nuts and cookies concluded our meal. The waiter then poured the mint teas as he did in the hand-washing ceremony. By the end of the evening I was shocked to discover Barbara ate like a Berber.

When the Rotary Club and the University of Leeds sent Barbara her acceptance letters along with her scholarship offer, she graciously declined.

42. Alien Encounters

The time had come for Barbara to meet my tribe. The thought of her meeting my family for the first time was more nerve racking than going on our first date.

"She's a Shiksa, (a non-Jewish girl)," I thought to myself.

"How will my family react or behave?"

"First impressions matter."

"How do I prepare her for this encounter?"

"What if she runs off screaming as soon as Lurch, Morticia or Cousin "IT" answers the door?"

I decided to invite Barbara to a Passover Seder at my parent's home in Granada Hills. The Passover holiday was rich in heritage and tradition. I thought it would be a good introduction to our culture. It was one of the few times my entire family gathered to celebrate together. My parents, sisters, brother in law, aunt, niece, cousins, and friends would all be there.

"What do you do on Passover?" she asked. "Are you sure I'm not going to stick out like a sore thumb?" She spoke with a raised eyebrow, wondering if she would not fit in.

"We open the door for Elijah the Prophet, and yell, let all who are hungry come and eat; and if you are hungry they let you in," I responded.

"No, really, what am I supposed to do?" she inquired.

"We sing songs in Hebrew, eat raw horseradish and gefiltah fish, then we read the Hagaddah, which is the story of our exodus from Egypt. Trust me, you'll fit right in," I said confidently. "It will be one of those experiences you will never forget, I promise. If they start speaking to you in Hebrew just say, *atem magzimim* every few minutes and they'll think you are fluent," I advised her.

"What does *atem magzimim* mean?" she asked.

"It means you are all exaggerating," I replied.

We agreed to drive separate cars, just in case Barb felt she needed to leave early. I was so nervous; I forget where my parents lived or how to get there. I drove around the same block three times before I figured out I was on the wrong street. Barbara must have thought I was an idiot. I think it was a subconscious reaction. My brain was telling me, "Don't take her there. When she sees your family, she's going to run for it."

When my Emmah answered the door she was dressed like a Bedouin. Vered and Emmah were both wearing abayas. These were loose unencumbered robes worn by Bedouin women. My mother's robe was made of black cut velvet fabric. Black was the dominant Bedouin color. Vered's robe was less traditional. Hers was made of red cut velvet fabric. The garments were long and ample with wide and deep sleeves. They were richly embellished with fine hand embroidery, which were stitched with golden threads. Vered's hair was dyed a bright orange-red from the henna she used. Henna is a green powder that smells like hay. The leaves of the henna plant have an orange-red dye, which stains hair the orange-red color. It's an ancient natural hair colorant used in the Middle East. Barb was staring at my sister's flaming hair and my mother's and sister's Bedouin robes and was just speechless.

"I told you, you're going to fit right in," I said sarcastically.

As soon as Barb walked in the house, she had to cover her ears. The decibel level was equivalent to a heavy-metal rock concert. To Barbara it appeared as though everyone in my family was yelling at one another. I told her they were just discussing things in Hebrew.

"It can get heated," I said, "but unless they start pulling out knives, they are just talking. They are not fighting, at least not yet."

I walked Barb around the house and introduced her to my family. "This is my sister Vered and her husband Pini, my Aunt Edna, and my cousin Shabtai and his wife Yael," I said nonchalantly, like these were normal people.

My cousin Shabtai went by the name Shaby. He was named after my great-grandfather, who was his grandfather. Shaby always disliked the Surname Mizrahi given to his family, so he changed it to Moore.

Shaby, I asked, "Is anyone waiting for you at home?"

"No, he said, "not that I am aware of."

Shaby never believed in schedules, and he didn't like telling anyone "Sorry I can't be there," or "Sorry, I have something else planned." If anyone wanted to visit Shabtai, he would say, "Sure come on over." When my cousin had to be somewhere else, and someone showed up at his house, he would just hand him a video and say, "watch this movie, and call me when it's done I should be back by then," and he would leave his house with this person standing there with a tape in his hands. My cousin would often have people sitting in his living room all alone, watching movies while he was somewhere else.

Other family members just walked up to Barbara and gave her a big hug. I could tell by her somewhat stunned and disoriented reaction that this was not something she was accustomed to. I told her Israelis are very demonstrative with their affection.

When Barb met Emmah, the first thing my mom asked to see was her hand. She wanted to read her palm, but when I saw what she was trying to do, I told Emmah, "Not now, maybe another time, like in our next life."

"Barb," I quickly said in a whispered tone and without much explanation, "it's our custom to rinse out our Turkish coffee cups as soon as soon as we finish drinking the coffee, especially before my mother gets hold of them."

Even though I did not allow my mother to assess Barbara by mysticism, she still fell in love with her instantly. My girlfriend was someone calm, rational, logical, intelligent, and not superstitious. They say opposites attract and Barbara and Jaffa were exact opposites.

When we came to Lily, my younger sister, she was busy watching Danielle, Vered's new infant daughter. Danielle was pulling on her hair.

Lily turned her head towards the baby and began yelling, "*die, die, die....*" Barbara's cheeks became flushed and she looked toward the front door of our house in the way a passenger on an airplane would look at an emergency exit. I had to explain to her, my sister was just telling the baby in Hebrew enough, enough, enough. *Die* in Hebrew means *enough.* "And by the way," I said, "you should probably know that in Hebrew—*he* means she, *who* means he, and *hem* means them."

My mother prepared an elaborate Passover table. It was surrounded by generations of my family. We ate symbolic foods prepared with recipes that were passed down through the ages. The Seder was a structured meal. *Seder* means order, and this was a meal served in a series of steps, with prayers, rituals and special dishes used to tell the Exodus story.

It began with matzah, which was unleavened bread symbolizing Jews' haste as they fled from Egypt. Something my ancestors did in Biblical times and my great-grandmother did again in the twentieth century. Then bitter herbs and charoset were served. The bitter herbs were a reminder of the bitterness of slavery, and charoset, which is a concoction of apples, nuts, honey and wine, represented the mortar used with the bricks we made as slaves. Then eggs in tears were served, which were hard-boiled eggs dipped in salt water.

Gefilte fish and chicken soup with matzah balls were also Passover staples. The main course was stuffed boneless chicken breast with apricot jam. It was served with a profusion of salads, roasted red peppers, and eggplant dishes. Dessert followed with a special unleavened Passover cake, chocolate covered matzahs, fruit and nuts.

There is a difference of opinion in Jewish tradition as to whether we are supposed to drink four or five cups of wine during the Seder. We follow the majority opinion of drinking only four cups, but in deference to the minority opinion, we pour a fifth cup of wine, even though no one drinks it. The fifth cup is set aside for Elijah the Prophet. In Judaism, it takes a prophet from the Biblical era to resolve our disputes. I'm sure one of these times when my family opens the door to welcome Elijah, he'll enter and ask, "What is it with you people? I could hear you arguing all the way up in heaven."

The Seder could easily have been Barb's and my Last Supper if things hadn't gone well. Prior to that evening, I was not sure Barbara would be able to straddle the divide between our cultures. To my surprise, not only was she able to make the leap, but she also seemed to be drawn to the exotic and unfamiliar. Barbara loved the food, the song and the warmth of my family.

43. Survival Of The Fittest

Barbara surprised me for my birthday. She planned a charming romantic weekend getaway for the two of us. "Don't worry about a thing, I have it all planned out," she said enthusiastically.

We drove to San Pedro and Barb purchased the round trip tickets on the Catalina Express, a water taxi to Catalina. A few times a day, the ferry crossed the twenty five-mile channel to Catalina Island, a preserve with rugged peaks and a dramatic coastline. We landed in the mythical town of Avalon, where we disembarked with our backpacks, sleeping bags and cooler. Avalon was a funky little beach town suspended in time. Only three thousand full-time inhabitants lived there. Cars were restricted and golf carts were the vehicles of choice to putt around in. But Barbara's plan didn't include a stay in Avalon.

"Camping is the most intimate way to enjoy Catalina's rugged beauty," she said. "It's also a lot less expensive than a hotel," she added.

The island was protected by the Catalina Conservancy, which made certain that Catalina forever remained in its natural state. The roads on this island were designed to be as non-invasive as possible. They were narrow, twisting, dusty and winding. The island was only eighteen and a half miles long and seven miles wide and was made up of many peaks and canyons. The highest peak rose 2,125 feet above sea level and was at the center of the island at the Blackjack Campground, the place we were headed to. To get to Blackjack, Barbara purchased two one way tickets on the Safari Bus. It took us to the trailhead at the campground. The site was nine bumpy miles from Avalon. From the trailhead it was another one-and-a-half-mile hike to the campsite. We got off the bus with our heavy backpacks and tied our sleeping bags to the frames of our packs. We each grabbed one of the handles on our cooler and started to hike side by side to the campsite.

As we hiked toward Blackjack, we encountered two college-aged couples sitting on their cooler. They had towels on their heads, which shielded their eyes from the sun. They were desperate for water. "We only have hard liquor. We'll trade you anything for some water," they muttered through their parched lips. We gave them a bottle of water and as we walked past them, I turned to Barb and said, "What idiots! How could they allow themselves to get stuck out in the middle of nowhere without proper provisions?"

The campground was in the interior of the island and was nestled among pine and eucalyptus trees. It had sweeping views of the rolling terrain down to the ocean below. We immediately saw buffalo with their massive heads wandering around the hills of our campsite. The bison were the offspring of fourteen buffalo from a herd brought over in 1924 for the use in the film *The Vanishing American*. Dove, quail, wild turkey, deer, fox, goats, and wild boar were all sighted at one time or another on the island.

When we arrived at the campsite, there was a posting by the outhouse stating, "Beware Dangerous Wild Boar." I've never been a fan of pigs. They are not kosher and these were not ordinary farmyard animals. Wild boars weighed four times as much as regular pigs. They had razor-sharp tusks and a temper. These were pigs with an attitude. They were very fast and aggressive and were known to charge people and gore them. There was no fence around the campground to protect us. I told Barb there was no way I was going to camp out in the open air only to be gored to death, or worse, have my face eaten off by an animal the size of a motorcycle that looked a lot like a prehistoric carnivore. Barb said she had a lot of camping experience and told me not to worry. But I was out of my element. Camping was not something we did in my family. We decided to put our sleeping bags on top of the metal picnic tables three feet off the ground. Even though it was very hot, I slept deep inside my sleeping bag with my head totally covered. No animal was going to bite my face off while I slept.

When the sun rose the next morning, I slowly stuck my neck out of the shell of my sleeping bag and made certain no animal was about to pounce on me. It was a beautiful morning and we were looking forward to the hike down to the beach.

As we were hiking Barbara turned to me and asked, "Do you have any cash left?"

"No," I said, "But I have a credit card on me. Why do you ask?"

"Well," she said hesitantly, "the round trip ferry ride and the bus ride to the campsite cost more than I expected. I only had enough money to purchase a one way ticket to the campsite."

"Are you telling me we don't have enough money to get back to Avalon?" I said astonished.

"It's about eleven miles from the camp site back to Avalon and we would need to carry our backpacks and cooler the whole way. Why didn't you let me pay for the ferry with a credit card?" I asked perturbed.

"Because this was my gift to you and I wanted it to be my treat," she said in a whispered tone.

I immediately thought of the three college guys without water willing to trade anything for what they needed. I asked Barb what we had left in the cooler. She said we had bread, water and a bag of oranges. I asked her how much we needed for the bus ride back. "We are five dollars short," she said. I then took the bag of oranges and offered to sell them to the other campers in Blackjack. After I described the situation we were in, and after they stopped laughing at me, I was able to get six bucks so we could get back to Avalon with a dollar to spare.

44. Moving In

By the time I was a senior year in college, Barbara and I had shared over six hundred meals together. Moving in, we thought, was the next natural step in our relationship.

"But, were we ready for it?"

"Would the things which were no longer unattainable be less desirable?"

"Would I enjoy watching her floss her teeth or clip her toenails?"

"Would we argue over leaving the toilet seat up or not taking out the trash?"

We started out as footloose companions and evolved. We were infatuated with one another and wanted to spend more time together. We wanted to be certain we were compatible before we made a lifelong commitment to each other.

Our apartment was in Westwood, deep in enemy territory, adjacent to our archrival school UCLA. They may have been our rivals, but they lived in the better part of town, and there was nothing they could do to stop USC students from living there. Bel Air, Beverly Hills, and Brentwood, some of the most affluent neighborhoods in California, bordered Westwood. There were several art deco movie palaces within walking distance from our place. A pedestrian oriented shopping area with numerous restaurants was close by, and a French pastry shop was just around the corner.

The complex we lived in was an amusement park. The elevator looked like a mineshaft. Its cab was made of metal mesh and had a glass wall at the back exposing what looked like a shaft dug out of rock. The Jacuzzi was in a large cave in an area adjacent to the pool. The pool had a black bottom and river rocks all around the perimeter. It looked like a natural stream with a pond in the middle. The garden area contained a huge human-sized birdcage with a bench in it as well as a labyrinth made of hedges.

The unit we rented was a tiny furnished studio apartment totaling approximately three hundred square feet. It had no bedroom. Our living room had a fold out sofa, which became our bed. The fake fireplace in the corner was made of plastic and had a red light bulb with tinsel which spun around the bulb creating a very bad illusion of fire. The carpeting looked like a putting green. Our kitchen could only fit one person at a time in it and the dining table could barely seat two people opposite one another. We had no bathtub and there was barely enough room for the shower. It was a very cozy place.

One of Barbara's conditions for living together dealt with our phone. She did not want me to answer it. Barbara decided, at least for the time being, to keep me a secret from her parents. It would drive me crazy to see the phone ring and ring and ring until Barb could get to it.

My parents knew we were serious about each other and were living together. The first gift Barbara received from my family was intimate apparel. My mother bought her a nightgown. There wasn't anything I could possibly do to shock my family.

I didn't know Barbara's parents. Much of how we communicate is learned from our families. I did not know if they were the types who would blab about her relationships to others. Maybe what they considered to be deep dark secrets were the typical dinner table discussions at my parents' house. But secrets can cause pain and come with enormous emotional costs. Keeping secrets was just too much work for my taste. I never understood why Barbara wanted to keep our relationship a secret. Was she afraid, embarrassed or ashamed? I didn't want to be the horrible dark thing people whispered about behind closed doors. I was just glad she finally told her parents about me.

45. The Oregon Trail

Barbara and I decided to trek up to Oregon to meet her parents. We arrived by airplane, but because I was anxious, the flight seemed as though it was never going to end. At least it wasn't as hard as traveling by covered wagon over the mountains and deserts of the Oregon-trail like the original settlers did.

Portland was a place where it rained in fall, winter, and spring and sometimes in the summer too. The rains feed the stately elms, firs and sycamore trees, which formed a green canopy wherever you looked. It was an emerald city made up of light green grasses and dark green trees and every other shade of green in between.

What immediately struck me about the locals was how rarely Oregonians use umbrellas. To look like a Portlander you run out to the nearest Columbia Sportswear shop and purchase a waterproof jacket. These were people who let the rain roll off their shoulders.

Portland was Oregon's biggest city, but even its biggest city had a cozy small town feel. Portlanders knew how to brighten up the dark and dreary rainy days. The streets of Portland were lined with bistros, coffee shops, bookstores, microbreweries, jazz clubs, and boutiques, all with bright interiors. Most places had fireplaces where you could warm up once you dried off. You could settle into a dry spot to sit and sip a cup of java and read a paper or book.

The pace of life here was slower. This city was a place where people took the time to stop and smell the flowers. Oregonians were bohemian, unpretentious, homogenous and liberal. The locals would never praise the place. Praise, according to their logic, would cause growth and development. Two words they dreaded the most.

Barbara's parents lived in a modest split-level home in a middle class neighborhood in North East Portland. The front and back yards rivaled any botanical or zoological venue I ever visited. Her father would regularly feed the raccoons, squirrels, birds, cats, ducks, and geese that inhabited their backyard. They had enormous sycamores, firs and weeping willows and what appeared to me to be every species of flowering plant known to man.

When her parents opened the front door I was relieved to find they were not dressed like Bedouins. Her mother, Marilyn, and her father, Victor, were both school teachers. Marilyn taught second graders and Victor taught in high school. They introduced themselves with their calm and polite school teacher voices and invited us in. No one gave me a great big bear hug when I entered, just a warm handshake. I knew I had to be on my best behavior and had to mind my P's and Q's.

The small vestibule at the entry of the split-level home led either upstairs or downstairs. Barbara was told she would be staying upstairs in her old room, and I was led downstairs into her brother's room. Ken was five years younger than Barbara and was going to be sleeping on the sofa while I visited.

As soon as they said, "You will be staying in Ken's room," I was struck by the fact Marilyn and Victor named their children after the Mattel Company dolls. They had a Ken and Barbie.

As I entered Ken's room, I immediately noticed a large framed poster on the wall of what appeared to be a rat. "What have I gotten myself into?" I wondered. "Maybe Ken saw the movie about the rat named Ben," I thought to myself. The movie was about a boy named Willard who forms a close bond with a giant rat the size of a cat. Willard finds the rat in his basement and discovers he can control him. He then trains Ben to attack people he dislikes.

"Did Ken have pet rats in the basement?"

"Why else would he have a framed picture of one?"

"Did he dislike me?"

No matter what the answers to my questions were, I knew I would have to sleep with one eye open and with the bed covers over my head. I also became concerned about what would happen if I got startled in the middle of the night. If I woke-up and saw the picture of the rat on the wall, how would they react to my screaming?

"Does Barbara's father have a gun?"

"Would they require me to seek professional help before I got to spend any more time with their daughter?"

When Vic saw me glaring at the poster he said, "It's an opossum." He could tell by the blank expression on my face I had never heard of an opossum. "It's a small, tree-dwelling American marsupial," he continued. I nodded my head like I now knew what he was talking about, but I had absolutely no clue. It still looked like a rat to me. All I knew was that I was going to be nodding my head a lot this weekend.

After settling into Ken's room in the basement, I went upstairs to the dining room. Barb's mother was putting out some snacks on the table while Ken, Victor and Barbara were discussing something and laughing. Ken then placed an acorn shaped fruit in front of me and asked if I have ever tried a persimmon.

To be precise he said, "Have you ever tried a Hachiya persimmon?"

"No, I said, "I don't believe I have."

"I'll eat the mushy one," he said. "You're our guest you can have the one that's not overripe."

As soon as I bit into the persimmon, they all began to laugh at my pucker. My whole body shook from the taste. It was the most sour and outrageously astringent fruit I had ever tried. Typically, the skin should be transparent and the fruit should be absolute mush before you eat it. The rotten one was actually sweet and had some interesting spicy notes to it. I now knew what they were plotting and laughing about in my absence. If I was going to survive this weekend, I knew I would have to be more vigilant.

Barb's younger brother was a brilliant high school student who loved science and physics. His speech was slow and deliberate. When he spoke, he paused after each word. It was like he was searching through a large data bank of vocabulary words and then selected just the right one before he spoke.

Later that morning Ken asked Barbara and me to join him for ride to the store. When we reached the iced-over vacant parking lot, Ken decided to demonstrate his understanding of Newton's three laws of motion.

Newton's first law was that every object in a state of uniform motion tends to remain in that state of motion unless an external force is applied to it. Ken decided to spin his car on the ice. Since we were heading in one direction when he began his spin, the vehicle continued to glide on the ice in the same direction of motion it was going before he began to spin it.

Newton's second law dealt with the relationship between an object's mass m, its acceleration a, and an applied force F. In Ken's case, the large mass of the car had a certain velocity when he began his spin, and a mass with a certain velocity will maintain that velocity unless a force acts on it to cause it to accelerate or decelerate. Since we were on a sheet of ice, Ken's attempts at slowing or stopping the car did not work. We would soon feel the force of the mass times the acceleration.

Finally Newton's third law stated that for every action there was an equal and opposite reaction. As we were skidding towards the wall of ice at the end of the shopping center, we knew our car would shortly bounce off the wall with a force equal to and opposite to the one we were sliding into it with.

When we returned from our errand, I asked for a glass of water, a Tylenol and grabbed the nearest chair to recover from this ordeal. I thought my family was strange. Hers could be outright dangerous. I wasn't certain I could survive getting to know the rest of her family.

Barbara's mother grew up in Butte, Montana. The state was the fourth largest in the country with 148,000 square miles, but had a population of only 900,000 people. Montana was a place where people stopped and chatted. It could take an hour to walk a single block in Butte. People stop to discuss the weather, their gardens, or the apple pie they just made. Even though nothing much changes from day to day, they still visit with each other and discuss the same three topics.

Marilyn saw the world through a second grade teacher's eyes. Second graders explore the world through their senses. Barb's mother would point things out like the sounds of the insects, or the colors of certain flowers, the feel of different textures, and what things taste like. But, since she had lost her sense of smell, she didn't discuss what things smelled like. She was very observant and aware of her environment. I always got the sense when I nodded approvingly or answered a question correctly I was shortly going to be receiving a treat, a sticker or a glittery gold star. Being around second graders was exhausting work. I have nothing but respect for the patience and kindness required of a teacher.

Victor Kaufmann was a ninth generation American. He grew up on a farm in Indiana and was educated in a single room schoolhouse. As a farm boy he received his first shotgun at the ripe old age of nine. Vic was an expert marksman and could shoot squirrels on the farm from great distances.

In December of 1942 the United States Army set up the Army Specialized Training Program ("ASTP") to identify, train and educate academically-talented enlisted men as a specialized corp of Army officers during World War II. The men of the ASTP were distinguished by an octagon shoulder patch with the insignia of the lamp of knowledge crossed with the sword of valor, an allusion to both the mental and physical capabilities of these special men. Victor had attended Yale for a semester before he went to into the infantry under this program. When the Army needed men on the battlefield they gave Vic the choice of joining the paratroopers, paragliders, or infantry. Since he was scared of heights, and the only option to stay on the ground was infantry, he chose the infantry.

While in Wurselen, Germany, not far from Holland border, on a cold and wet night, the Germans blew up the row house the American soldiers were staying in. The explosion collapsed the entire first floor onto the cellar where the soldiers were sleeping. After clearing the debris, the surviving soldiers climbed out of the cellar, and the squad leader moved the men towards the valley in front of them with the hills to their left. As the infantrymen walked perpendicular to the hills, German machinegun fire mowed them down. Victor was wounded by one bullet that went into his left leg above his knee and a second bullet which ricocheted off of his bayonet and went into his shoulder. As Vic lay face down in the cold damp earth, the Germans were walking around checking the dead. He expected to die that day. He had been lying there for many hours and was now at peace with the fact he had done the best he could. Then all of a sudden the area began to be shelled with 155MM proximity fuse artillery. This ordinance detonated at the most favorable position to inflict the maximum damage to the area and it caused the Germans to flee. With Vic's ear close to the ground he heard the rumbling of tanks coming toward him. Not knowing if they were American tanks or German tanks he remained face down and motionless; motionless, that is, until a soldier grabbed him and turned him over. As Vic looked up he saw the face of a friend from Spokane, Washington, looking down at him with tears in his eyes. Victor was sent to a hospital in Birmingham, England to recover. When his wounds healed, he chose to be sent back to his platoon in Germany. I'm not sure whether Victor Kaufmann was the luckiest or unluckiest man alive. But this gentle man was awarded both the Silver Star and a Purple Heart. After the War, Victor completed his Yale education on the G.I. bill.

Victor met Marilyn in Montana while he was an insurance adjuster. Montana is where I believe Vic acquired his unique driving skills. I could now see a pattern with regards to the Kaufmanns' driving. Only one word adequately described it—terrifying. You could drive in Montana for hours and not see another car on the interstate. Most places were at least an hour away in between the mountains, farms, prairies, small towns and the cities he had in his territory. It was an immense open space where someone could drive as aggressively as one wished. Vic drove as fast and furiously as he liked, and he liked speed. It didn't matter if he was driving around windy craggy peaks or across vast grassy hills. It didn't matter if he was driving through a powerful winter storm or if it was a clear hot summer day, he drove perilously. There were only a few insurance-adjusting emergencies which required speed, but most didn't. One emergency was when he got a call from a man who lit a cigarette while he was in an outhouse. The outhouse exploded, and Vic had to get there quickly to see it for himself.

But now Victor was an English high school teacher. He had to deal with the hormonal teens, chaperone their dances, and grade their papers. In his spare time he would love to garden. Both Vic and Barbara were happiest when their hands were immersed in dirt. This father and daughter possessed a special farming gene. They both enjoyed going to their gardens alone. They went there to sit, think, and plant things. It was their little patch of paradise. When Barbara and her father looked at land they thought about what they could plant in it. When I looked at a piece of land I thought about what I could build on it. They loved land for land's sake. I loved land because I enjoyed knowing that I could profit from it. Vic and Barbara could get into long and gratifying discussions about horticulture. Given the fact I wouldn't know a weed from a plant, I never understood a word they were saying. I would just sit there and nod.

"Dad," she would say, "your rhododendrons are beautiful this year."

"Thank you." he said, "Did you see my *hemerocallis flava*?"

To me it sounded like he was telling her he was recently diagnosed with something bad, but then Barb said, "The day lilies are gorgeous." It was nice to see Barbara and her father spoke the same language, even if it was a language I couldn't speak.

When Victor asked me to take a walk with him the next evening, I was concerned I was about to get the speech about how he owned a gun and a shovel, and how he knew how to use both of them. Or worse, I was afraid he was going to bring up our religious and cultural differences. Victor Kaufmann was a man of German ancestry. He and Marilyn were Methodists. He had seen first hand what hatred towards Jews looked like. He could have said, "You can't marry my daughter. The chasm between us is too large. Our cultures are alien to one another. It will never work." But Vic did nothing of the sort. Instead, he said one of the kindest things any potential father-in-law could tell a son-in-law. He said, "I am not worried about Barbara any more. Knowing she's with you makes me feel certain she will be well cared for."

46. Ruth

The odd thing about Judaism is being a Jew has nothing to do with what you believe or what you do. A person born to a non-Jewish mother who has not undergone the formal process of conversion, but who believes everything an Orthodox Jew believes, and observes every law is still not a Jew. On the other hand, a person born to a Jewish mother, who is an atheist, is considered a Jew. Unlike other faiths, being Jewish is more like citizenship than a religion. But once a person obtains "legal citizenship" through conversion, they are as much of a Jew as anyone born Jewish. Religion was a topic Barbara and I rarely discussed while we were dating, but as our relationship matured, it became a subject we gave some thought to."I've decided to take a Jewish conversion class at the University of Judaism. But I'm not taking the class to convert, I'm taking it to learn," she said. Barbara, whose Scottish ancestors were members of the McDougal clan, was interested in the tribe of Judah.

"Why?" I asked. "You know, you don't need to take classes to please me."

"If I study something, it's for my sake, not yours. I want to understand more about your background," she said flatly.

Barbara always had an inquisitive mind. She intuitively understood, way before I did, how important these issues are in a relationship. The University was part of the conservative branch of Judaism. It was on Mulholland Drive, high on a bluff overlooking Los Angeles and had an incredible view of the city lights. Barbara loved the setting.

"How was your class?" I'd ask.

"I like the fact Judaism allows for critical examination. What's important is the here and now, and the whole concept of repairing this world in a proactive manner seems very reasonable to me. Judaism is a way of life, complete with a defined set of beliefs and practices, and I find it appealing." she said.

"I was always allowed to question my Rabbis about what didn't make sense to me. How does that compare to what Methodists do?" I asked.

"Look," Barb said, "My mother and I went to church, because that's what we did, and I didn't question it. My dad rarely, if ever, went to church. He's more of an agnostic. You and I both believe in the same one G-d, the only thing I really need to adjust, if I become Jewish, is the belief Jesus was not the Messiah, and since certain things didn't happen after Jesus came, it isn't difficult for me to believe he wasn't the Messiah."

"When the Messiah does eventually come, we can then ask him, 'Is this your first visit or is this your second visit?' I said sarcastically, having heard this line before. "At least Jews don't send non-believers to hell if they are not Jewish. We believe there is a place in Heaven for all righteous people, even if they are not Jewish, and only righteous Jews go to heaven, not all Jews."

Between the time Barbara started her classes at the University of Judaism and completed them, we decided to get engaged. I didn't even get the chance to ask her to marry me, she asked first. She made me my favorite breakfast, matzah and eggs, and she just blurted out, "So are we going to ever get married?" Not exactly the most romantic proposal in the world, but it worked.

Barbara decided she would convert, but the debate over who was considered a Jew and the laws regarding the right of return to Israel affected our decision. Orthodox Jews do not accept the authority of Conservative, Reform or Reconstructionist rabbis to perform conversions. The Conservatives don't accept the Reform movement's and Reconstructionists' conversions. The Orthodox rabbis were the ones setting the rules for Israel, and since no other branch of Judaism questioned their conversions, or children of those converts, Barbara decided she would be converted by an Orthodox rabbi, and decided to not complete the conversion at the University of Judaism, which was Conservative. She wanted her credentials as a Jew to be beyond reproach.

It is traditional for a rabbi to turn a potential convert away three times before agreeing to convert the individual. By doing this the rabbis are trying to determine a convert's sincerity. The process generally lasts a year and could even be longer, and even though Barb went through the classes at the Conservative University, the Orthodox rabbis would begin the process all over again.

Our first step was to contact a rabbi. We were referred to an Orthodox rabbi who did conversions, but not one any of my family knew personally. I told Barbara I would join her for all of her classes, since I needed a refresher on religion also. But in reality, all I wanted to do was make certain she wasn't just getting one person's view. Jews always have more than one opinion, and I wanted to make sure she heard my opinion as well.

The rabbi's office was in a small retail store front in Los Angeles. It was run by an organization called Chabad. As we walked into the office, we saw an elderly, unkept man, who had a dour look on his face as if he had just eaten something bad. He began by asking Barbara short, curt questions like, "Where are you from?" "Why do want to convert?"

I could tell he wasn't even listening to her answers. He just wanted to dissuade Barbara from converting no matter what she said. The rabbi could see Barbara was uncomfortable; her voice was shaky and her hands had a slight tremble, but he kept trying to find her soft spot.

"You know, if you are Jewish, you have to give up your Christmas tree," he said tersely. "No Santa Claus is ever going to come down your chimney again," he continued half mockingly.

"I'm fine with that," Barbara responded.

"And you know you will never be able to see your parents or family again," he said in a low-pitched growl.

Barbara's face began to contort and the tears began flowing down her cheeks. I could tell he wasn't going to stop; he was like a maggot on a dead carcass and seemed to be enjoying himself.

I told Barbara what he was saying wasn't true. Trying to dissuade someone from converting was one thing, but he was just plain mean. There is a special commandment to love and be kind to converts, even more than ordinary Jews (Devarim 10:19). Even though she wasn't a convert yet, he was going way beyond determining if she was sincere. Barbara didn't look Jewish, she wasn't born Jewish, and she had a very different background from typical Jews, and it was obvious her alien features were at the forefront of this man's words and actions.

We decided not to go back to this rabbi ever again. Instead, we found a kind, wonderful rabbi named Joseph Feinstein, who never resorted to cruelty to dissuade Barb from becoming a convert. He taught us for approximately a year before agreeing to send Barbara to the Bet Din, or Jewish court, in Los Angeles. After asking Barb a lot of detailed questions the Bet Din then completed the conversion, but there were two final steps. The first one was selecting a Hebrew name, and the second was an immersion in a mikveh, or ritual bath.

Barbara chose the Hebrew name Ruth. Ruth the Moabite in the Torah was Judaism's most important convert. She was the great-grandmother of King David, and according to the Old Testament the Messiah will be a direct descendant of Ruth's.

47. Road Scholar

I went from being an awkward, lowly freshman, to a seasoned senior in nothing flat. It seemed that quick. After completing all of my general education requirements, courses in finance, marketing, accounting, communications and organizational behavior, I felt like I was ready for the real world. When I started business school I didn't know which side a debit or credit went on, and now I was going to be a Certified Public Accountant. I chose accounting, not because it was a subject I loved, but because it was the secure thing to do. I wanted a life where my hands would always be clean and a life where I was guaranteed rock-solid stability. A CPA designation equated to a guaranteed job. Accounting was a portable profession. All I needed was a pencil and I was in business. Now it was time for me to hit the road and take ownership of my life and career.

Businesses had everything I could possibly want, drama, comedy, tragedy, influence, and power. It was all about who came out on top? Who got screwed? Who got lucky or unlucky? It was also about being in the right place at the right time?

I was just a poor schmuck who was determined to become a rich prick. To me money wasn't the root of all evil. The lack of money was. Needing money was what led most people to make bad decisions. Having to worry about money was terrible. Since I did not come from a wealthy family, I was always worried. It was something I no longer wished to do. Accounting would be my ticket to a better life. The foundation of any business was built on its finances.

Knowing how to read financial statements was as rudimentary to a businessman as an architect knowing how to read a blueprint.

A top-level accountant wasn't a rumpled man who wore green eyeshades anymore. If I got hired by one of the first-tier firms, known as the Big Eight, I would become an advisor to Fortune 500 companies as well as the rich and famous. The cream of the accounting field worked for these eight firms. They represented the world's largest public accounting companies.

Emmah, a typical Jewish mom, wanted me to become either a lawyer or doctor. I don't know why, but accounting was never a profession viewed with the same level of esteem as a doctor or lawyer. My mother begged Barbara to promise her she would make me go to law school. Barbara told my mother, "Your son's a big boy; he can make his own decisions. I'm not his wife and I'm not in a position to dictate his life to him. Well, at least not yet."

It wasn't enough to be a technical geek; the Big Eight firms were looking for hard-working and hard-playing individuals who knew the technical aspects of the profession and who could also be rainmakers, which were the people who brought in the business. They wanted people who could communicate and interface with clients and sell them their services.

The accounting honor society at USC, Beta Alpha Psi, hosted a dinner for its top students and invited all of the recruiters from the Big Eight and the national and local firms. I sat at a table with Jeff Palmer, the head recruiter from Peat, Marwick, Mitchell & Co., currently called KPMG. The firm employed nearly 94,000 people worldwide, provided audit, tax and advisory services in 717 cities and 148 countries and was one of the largest of the Big Eight. Jeff looked more like a model athlete than an accountant. He loved to play mind games with the potential recruits. Jeff already knew the students at the dinner had the grades needed to be hired by his firm. He wanted to know how they reacted under pressure.

I went to the restroom and when I came back, Jeff Palmer, turns to me and says, "I spoke with Suchi Lee, your debate partner, and he tells me you're gay."

I turned to him with a smirk on my face and said, "Suchi heard being gay was an asset at Peat Marwick. My friends would say anything to help me get a great job." I knew being a wise guy would either get me the job or prevent me from getting one. There was no middle ground. Mr. Palmer was pushing the boundaries. I just pushed back. If he had done the same thing in today's politically correct environment, I'm certain KPMG would be sued, but back then it was just horseplay.

The next day Jeff Palmer set up a formal interview for me on the forty-second floor of the Bank of America Tower in Downtown, Los Angeles. It took over one minute in the elevator to get up to the forty-second floor. As I was getting higher and higher in the building, it struck me that we were in Los Angeles and earthquakes were not uncommon in downtown. I thought to myself, "What would I do if I were on the forty-second floor during an earthquake?"

One of my friends at USC my junior year was Sam Sinasohn. He was a year older than I was, and Peat Marwick had hired him a year earlier. Peat Marwick always used the most recent graduates to interview potential new hires and Sam was assigned to me. Recent graduates still knew who the top students were at the University they had just graduated from. They also knew if that person would fit into their organization.

One of the first questions I asked Sam was, "Are you ever concerned about working on the forty second floor of this building?

"Not really," He said nonchalantly.

"What would happen if we have an earthquake?" I asked.

"The building moves," was his response.

"What do you mean the building moves?" I said astonished.

"Well, they built the tower on wheels or springs. The building moves with the earth, so it shouldn't collapse during an earthquake. On windy days the building sways back and forth. It's a little eerie sometimes. They recommend you sit a few feet away from the glass exterior walls in case the building starts moving."

I nodded like it was O.K. If Sam wasn't worried, why should I.

The rest of my interview with Sam consisted of a three-hour lunch, a few cocktails, a bottle of fine wine, and comparing notes on our girlfriends. Two days later, I received my first job offer from Peat Marwick Mitchell & Co., and I accepted it.

To get a CPA certificate, in addition to having a college degree and two years of specific accounting experience, which I was going to receive at Peat Marwick and Mitchell, accountants needed to pass a rigorous two-day, four-part exam. Less than one quarter of the candidates who took the exam passed it. In California, if someone passed two parts of the exam initially, one only needed to retake the other two parts within a certain period of time to pass the entire exam.

Taking and passing the CPA exam was the next hurdle I needed to jump. The amount of data I needed to be proficient in was overwhelming. It was information overload. Studying for this exam entailed months of note taking, flash card preparation, mnemonic device memorization, and an understanding of testing strategies.

On the day of the exam I entered the Los Angeles convention center, where rows and rows of tables were set up on the main floor. Over two thousand accountants were taking the exam at this one location. I felt a little light-headed. I was up late the night before going over last minute lists and flash cards. My palms were sweaty and my heart was racing.

Shortly we would start a marathon exam, which lasted sixteen hours over a two-day period. I sat next to a gentleman who appeared to be in his forties. He introduced himself and said, "I remember what the exam was like when I was your age. There were far fewer financial accounting standards twenty years ago."

I looked at him with my head cocked to one side, a surprised look on my face, and said, "What do you mean you remember what the exam was like twenty years ago?"

He looked at me and said, "I've taken this dammed thing over twenty times. I haven't been able to pass it yet. But I'm pretty confident number twenty-one will be my magic number."

Chills ran down my back. I don't remember getting up, but suddenly I'm standing. I felt a tingling blush in my cheeks and acid from my stomach coming up my esophagus. I asked the exam proctor if I could go to the bathroom. I thought I was going to pass out. He told me I could go to the restroom, but the exam would start shortly, and I would not receive any extra time. I ran to the bathroom, leaned over one of the toilets, and began to vomit. I spent the first twenty minutes of the CPA exam puking. When I got back to my chair, my hands were still trembling. I tried to regain my composure, but I was totally psyched out. I had to really think hard about what my name was and how to fill in the bubbles on the computer form.

I was not surprised when I did not pass the CPA exam on my first try. But since I passed two sections, I only had to study for half of the exam the second time around. When I took the exam the next time, I didn't talk to anyone. Two ended up being my magic number.

48. A Soul Squelching Job

The starting annual salary for a tax department staff accountant in 1983 was twenty one thousand dollars. The cost to park in the same building as the world's largest accounting firm was two hundred dollars per month, or 11.428 percent of the basic pretax staff salary. It was a good thing Barbara was earning more than I was at the time. I don't think I could have survived on my measly income.

In order to conserve funds Sam Sinasohn and I decided we would car pool to work and split the fuel and parking costs. Sam arrived at my apartment each morning at 7:00 A.M. We both wore dark suits, white shirts with button down collars, and conservative colored ties. Peat Marwick had a strict dress code, and we all ended up looking like clones of each other. On the way to work, Sam and I would stop for breakfast at an L.A. institution called the Pantry on Figueroa Street. The restaurant had been open continuously since 1924. For six decades it operated twenty-four hours a day. There was no key to the front door of this well worn establishment. The line for breakfast would go out the door and down the street, but since it moved quickly, we would be seated and served in no time. As soon as we walked through the door, the odor of grease permeated the place. Most of the elderly waiters had worked there thirty or more years. They wore white shirts with black bow ties and black pants. Cesar, one of our regular waiters, would greet Sam and me by name. Before we could say good morning, he had mugs of coffee in front of us. The menu was plastered on the wall. All we had to do was place our order once we were seated at the Formica-covered tables, and within five minutes we were served. All of the portions were huge and we would alternate between the stacks of hotcakes or eggs with greasy hash browns. Being accountants, we loved to calculate how much this business made on a typical day. Even though they only had eight-four seats, the waiters told us they served between two thousand to three thousand people daily. According to the booklet by the cashier, the Pantry went through ninety tons of bread, seven thousand head of cattle, seven hundred and fifty thousand eggs, three thousand hogs, and two hundred and eight tons of potatoes each year. We estimated their net pretax profit to be in the neighborhood of six thousand dollars per day or $2,190,000 per annum.

After breakfast it was critical for us to get to the office within fifteen minutes or less. The Pantry's greasy hash browns acted like the dietary fiber in Metamucil. When we got stuck in traffic on the way to our office we would panic. Sam would shout and scream at the other vehicles as we rushed to the Bank of America Tower. We then had to go up the elevators to the forty-second floor before we ran straight for the restrooms.

In the first year, staff accountants start off with intensive training. Peat had dedicated training centers with full-time educational staff, and they employed nationally renowned experts who conducted their training. The main reason one wanted to work for a firm like Peat Marwick was the exposure to the top professionals in the industry.

Staff accountants who completed their preliminary training were paired up with senior associates. A staff accountant's career often depended on what kind of senior they were paired with. I was fortunate enough to get Phillip Holthouse as my mentor. Phil was one of the most respected seniors/managers in the office. He received the highest score in the state of California on his CPA exam. Phil spent a lot of time getting me up to speed and showing me the ropes. If

Phil hadn't taken me under his wing, I am not certain I could have survived the first year.

Other managers were not as kind or helpful. Computers were just starting to be used so most of the work was done by hand. One of the first hand prepared spreadsheets I completed for a manager appeared on my desk in shreds with a note stating I need to redo it. "The next time it needs to be legible!" was written on the note. Public Accounting firms all had an "up or out" attitude in their retention practices. One was either promoted or fired, there was no middle ground. The pressure was enormous. Within two years most of the staff members I started out with were no longer with the firm.

One quickly learned an hour worked was not the same as an hour earned. Staff accountants were given budgets to complete tasks based on the number of hours it took to complete the previous year. Managers and partners could only charge a client a certain set amount, so it was imperative the jobs were completed within the allotted time budget. Seniors who reviewed the work were concerned with it being correct, regardless of how long it took to complete the task. Staff accountants were always caught in the middle between perfection and expediency. The only way to achieve both objectives was to work ten to twelve hours a day and charge the clients account for eight to ten hours.

Interviewing new hires was one of the only true fun tasks a staff accountant had during the first year. Since all of the candidates we interviewed were already prescreened based on their grades, we really had very little more to go on other than instinct.

I decided to incorporate two new tests for potential hires. They were the French onion soup test and the salt tests. All recruits were taken out to lunch at the French restaurant on the first floor of the Bank of America Tower. The restaurant had a great French onion soup consisting of an inch-thick layer of baked cheese on top of the bread floating on the soup. It was impossible to eat the cheese without either using a knife or being stuck with long spaghetti-like strands hanging off the soup spoon. One could twirl the cheese around for days and still not run out of it. I loved to recommend the French onion soup to new hires. Watching them try to figure out how to eat the cheese under what I am sure were stressful circumstances in a very formal environment was always amusing. The smart ones would just push the cheese down below the soup, eat the onion soup and skip the cheese. The women I interviewed usually figured how to eat their soup the quickest. The men were determined not to give up on the cheese, and they would pull the cheese up and cut it with their knife or they would keep twirling the cheese on their spoon for our entire lunch. Either way I got to see them problem-solve.

The second test had to do watching people salt their food. Some candidates would always salt their food before tasting it. These people always baffled me. This particular restaurant always used a lot of salt in their cooking and the recruits would make an assumption about their food before they tasted it. I always felt this trait was a bad one for an auditor to have. Auditors should never prejudge or make assumptions about anything without knowing what they were getting into. I could never recommend someone who salted their food before tasting it.

49. Marriage

Barb and I announced we were getting married. I had a job and had passed the CPA exam. Barb was graduating from USC. We felt it was time to move forward and formalize our relationship.

What was interesting was how everyone started to give us advice after we announced our engagement. I was told by our Rabbi, "You can't be an accountant and a husband. When you are married, you can't keep track of who gave or did what and when, and then call for an audit when you disagree about something. Marriage isn't a business partnership. It's not give and take. It's give and give some more."

Then, I was told a story by a friend. It was about a couple who were married for fifty years. The husband had an annoying habit of leaving his toothpaste cap off of the tube each day, and every day his wife would tell him how annoying this was to her. Knowing this annoyed the heck out of his wife, for his fiftieth anniversary gift to his wife, he made a resolution that he would put the cap back on the toothpaste tube. So the husband starts each day and puts the cap back on. Day one goes by and his wife says nothing. Day two goes by and still she says nothing. Five days and then six days go by, and nothing is said. Finally he sees his wife is really angry with him, so he asks her, "Honey, what's wrong?" She turns to him and says "You know you are really becoming unbearable. Six days have gone by and you haven't brushed your teeth. It's absolutely disgusting." Then my friend looked at me and said, "Don't assume anything in a marriage. Make certain you communicate."

"Never go to bed angry," my sister said. I think this rule really only applies to women though. Women should never go to bed angry. Men can fall asleep even when they are angry. This special talent seems to make women even angrier. Men have the ability to go to sleep no matter what, and women just can't.

"Once the dress has been worn and the ring is on their finger, they turn into blow fish. They balloon to ten times their original size. Just wait and see....," a bachelor friend of mine warned.

Another friend told me "When they say for better or worse, make certain you ask yourself how worse is worse?"

Even after all of these words of wisdom, we decided to proceed with our plans. The notion of having Rabbi Feinstein marry us at Beth Jacob Synagogue in Beverly Hills, and then driving to our reception party on the Sundowner yacht in Marina Del Rey at sunset, sounded very romantic. But notions and the best laid plans don't always turn out as expected.

August 4, 1985, was a beautiful day in sunny California. Pini came to our apartment early in the morning, and began working on Barbara's hair. A professional makeup artist showed up an hour later to make certain my bride was camera-ready by noon. Barbara then put on her elegantly tailored gown and shoes and was ready for her close up.

All I had to do was put on my rented black tuxedo, since a green velvet tux was not available, and then pop in my contact lenses for the first time. I practiced this procedure at my optician's office several times, and it seemed easy with him right next to me. But things were totally different on my own. I had a feeling of trepidation when I tried putting the first lens in. I was always squeamish about eyeballs, especially my own, and the thought of me poking my eye out on my wedding day made me a little nervous. I washed my hands and dried them off and then put the first lens on my index finger of my right hand. Then I put a drop of solution in the center of the lens. With my left hand I tried to pull down my lower eyelid with my thumb and then looked up, just like the optometrist told me. But each time I tried to insert the lens my eye would reflexively close and knock the lens out of my hand. Then I needed to start the whole process over again. I nearly went mental trying to get my lenses in. I poked my eyes so many times they were now bright red. I couldn't stop blinking or rubbing them because it felt like they were on fire. I also couldn't stop tearing. It looked like I'd been crying all day. I decided to wear contact lenses instead of glasses on my wedding day so our pictures wouldn't have the glare from the photographer's flash in them from my eyeglasses. It was the one vain thing I was going to do, and now I looked like a tree frog with bulging, evil-looking, and red, glowing eyes.

When we got to Beth Jacob Synagogue, Rabbi Feinstein, my father and father-in-law to be, plus two male witnesses went into the Rabbi's private study to sign the Ketubah, or the Jewish marriage contract. The contract was written in Aramaic and since I was bleary-eyed and my Aramaic was a little rusty, I'm not certain what exactly it was I was signing. In an orthodox ceremony, no women are present for the Ketubah signing, and the bride does not need to sign this document, since it becomes her property. The Ketubah is all about the brides legal rights and her willingness to take part in the marriage, but she never has to sign it, which never made sense to me. Our Ketubah called for my bride, or her family, to pay the groom a dowry of twenty zuzzim. A zuz was an ancient Hebrew silver coin and was worth a fourth of a shekel. A zuz in the first century was also the average wage earned in a day. I never received any zuzzim, and since I never received my consideration, which is a key element of any binding contract, I'm not really bound to it by law.

While I was signing away my life, my bride was seated in the center of a separate room in a large chair. She was like a queen on her throne at the center of attention. Both fathers and the rabbi led me into the next room along with all male and female members of the immediate family for the b'deken, or veiling ceremony. The b'deken ceremony is a result of our forefather Jacob who was presented with a veiled bride whose face he could not see, and was thereby tricked into marrying the wrong woman, Leah. He had worked for Rachel for seven years, but was given Leah instead, and after the wedding night, it was too late to return the goods.

At my wedding, after checking my bride's face to make sure I was getting the right woman, I lowered the veil over her face and escorted her to the chuppah, or wedding canopy. The entire wedding party was already on the stage alongside the chuppah. The bridesmaids were my sister Lily, my cousin Nancy Mossberg, Barbara's cousin Debbie Slauson, and Sue Chognard, who was her maid of honor. Vered was asked to be a bridesmaid, but was pregnant with her second child David, and did not want to wear a bridesmaid's dress with her huge protruding belly. My groomsmen were Bill Kearney and Howard Newmark from my high school days, Sam Sinosohn, and Kevin Hyman, who was my best man, both from USC, and Norm Yoder a friend from Peat Marwick and Mitchell. I had asked my oldest friend David Ackerman to be my best man, but he could not make the trip to California at the time. Danielle, Vered's daughter was our flower girl.

As I looked over to my right, I noticed how funny the large white yarmulke looked on my father-in-law's head. There he was, smartly dressed in a black tuxedo, with a white yarmulke that just didn't sit right on his head; you could tell he wasn't used to wearing one. Vic was kind enough to wear one as a sign of respect, but it still looked odd to me. My mother and Marilyn, Barbara's mother, both wore what looked like matching light pink dresses and small pink hats. There we were, all standing under the chuppah, one big happy multicultural family. The chuppah itself dates back to the tent-dwelling days in the desert and represents a home. The original meaning of *chuppah* is to cover with garlands, and ours was covered with beautiful flowers by Violet Sinasohn, my friend Sam's mother. Violet did all of the flower arrangements for our wedding. Since I paid for the wedding and did not have a lot of extra funds at the time, I did not spend much on flowers. Violet ignored the limited amount of flowers we ordered, and went all out with the arrangements. It really made our chuppah special.

When the couple first enters the chuppah, the bride circles the groom seven times, representing the seven wedding blessings, the seven days of creation, and also, to remind the bride that the groom is the center of her world. From time to time I need to ask Barb to walk around me seven times to remind her Copernicus and Galileo were wrong: I'm the center of her solar system, not the sun.

The Kidushin, or the betrothal ceremony was next. It begins with greetings and a blessing over a cup of wine. The bride and groom drink from the same cup of wine, symbolically affirming that throughout life they will experience both joy and sorrow together. Following the blessing, the couple exchanges rings. Traditionally, the rings are solid and free of precious stones to avoid misrepresentation of its value (I guess in ancient times there were a lot of charlatans). Then a biblical verse from the Song of Songs is read, followed by the reading of the Ketubah. Finally, the actual wedding ceremony takes place with the chanting of the seven blessings. They consist of praise for G-d and the creation of the universe, a prayer for peace in Jerusalem, and good wishes for the couple. Upon completion of the blessings, the couple drinks from a second cup of wine and the ceremony concludes with the groom breaking a glass. Shattering glass reminds us to temper life's joyous moments with sober thoughts representing the destruction of the Temple in Jerusalem. Jews know life is not all joy; the happiness of the wedding day does not continue indefinitely.

With the conclusion of the ceremony, and the playing of "Erev Shel Shosanim" or "Evening of Roses" by our classical quartet, we were led to the Yihud room, or seclusion room. Immediately after the ceremony, the newly married couple retreats to a private room for fifteen minutes of personal time. In ancient times, the bride and groom would go to a nearby tent and actually consummate the marriage. Barbara and I seized this moment to eat, and we fed each other cakes and cookies before we were off to our floating wedding reception in Marina Del Rey.

Our ship was leaving the dock in Marina Del Rey promptly at 5:00 PM. All of the guests were given maps of where to park and how to get to the special dock in the Marina for our yacht. But my father, who was nervous and not thinking straight, ignored the directions and parked in the main marina area which had limited parking spaces and was at least a half mile away from where The Sundowner was docked. Since my father drove one of the lead cars, many guests followed him to the wrong area and had to fight for a parking space and then run to the boat to make it in time. My cousin Tommy, Sima's son, was left at the dock. When we heard screaming and saw him waving his arms wildly at the dock, the boat was steered back to pick him up. Other guest arrived winded and frustrated, so I made certain they had something to drink right away. The Sundowner had three levels. The lower level had the bed-rooms and a large living area. The center level had a bar and large entertaining area and dining tables set up for the hundred guests aboard. The top of the boat had a DJ and a bar. The different decks ended up being segregated by age. Older guests stayed on the lower decks and the younger crowd headed straight for the bar on the top deck. Kevin Hyman toasted us; he said he saw a bumper sticker on a car on the way to the dock, and he said it must have been an omen. The sticker said, "Live, Love and Laugh." I'm really glad he didn't see a "Save the Whales" bumper sticker. I can only imagine what that toast would have been like.

As Barbara and I watched the golden sunset from the bow of the Sundowner on that clear August night, our guests kept partying until the boat returned to the dock after dark. The younger guests seemed to love the experience of a cruise, while a few of the older guests said they felt seasick and couldn't wait to get back. Any time someone tries something unconventional, it seems impossible to please everyone. We were happy and couldn't wait to start our lives together and I wasn't going to let a few older fuddy-duddies ruin my wedding day, even if one or two of them needed to barf over the side of the boat.

The next day we were off on our honeymoon. I had accumulated two months of paid vacation in overtime working at Peat, Marwick & Mitchell and we were going to spend it traveling throughout Western Europe and Israel.

50. with Children

Four years after we ate the icing on our cake and shook the rice out of our hair, Barbara was pregnant. She looked great and felt pretty good throughout her first pregnancy. We were living in Thousand Oaks, California, and chose AMI Tarzana Regional Medical Center as our hospital and Dr. Peter Rubenstein as our obstetrician. Barbara and I took the requisite childbirth classes that were offered for free by the hospital. They used the Harris Method, instead of the Lamaze Method, for prepared child birthing. I always thought childbirth was a natural process. I never really got the reasoning behind classes. Most of what we were taught were breathing exercises, something I never really practiced until I had a class on how to do it. So I sat on the floor on a pillow next to my wife, in a room full of very pregnant hormonal wives and nervous husbands, and we practiced breeeeeeaaathing, breeeeeeeeaaaathing veeeery deeeeply, at least until we felt lightheaded.

I'm not certain when childbirth became a public affair or when fathers demanded to be present in the delivery room. Personally, I think some doors should be left shut. Whoever made it fashionable to swing the delivery door open was a moron. Typically, anything involving blood, heavy anesthetics, and screaming by someone you love should be avoided. But Barbara wanted me in the delivery room, and at the time it seemed like the thing to do. I miss the days when a father's role in the birthing process was limited to getting the mom to the hospital, pacing in the waiting room, and handing out the proverbial cigars. Now delivery rooms in some hospitals have spectator sections and the obstetricians act more like umpires than physicians. I understand childbirth is one of the only happy events to take place in a hospital, but I prefer to leave labor and delivery off my list of spectator sports.

On June 21st Barbara seemed restless and didn't sleep well, but she went to work at Litton Guidance and Control the next morning anyway. At about noon on June 22nd she felt labor pains, drove herself to the hospital, and was admitted. Later in the day she remembered to call me.

The delivery room at Tarzana hospital seemed very homey. It had light pink and blue wallpaper, furniture for guests to sit in, and had an apartment feel to it. Both Dr. Rubenstein and I wore matching green medical scrubs. I stood by Barbara's head, held her hand, and fed her ice chips, while Dr. Rubenstein sat at the other end of the bed. The doctor and I were having a nice conversation about USC football, with an intermittent "push," from the Doctor. That is until Barbara sat up and yelled at the two of us to "Just shut up already." The room was then relatively quiet other than her grunting and yelling until our baby was born.

Our daughter entered the world with a high-pitched cry at 9:16 PM on June 22, 1989. She weighed six pounds eight and a half ounces and was nineteen inches long. After counting all of her toes and fingers, the doctor gave her a perfect ten on her first test, called an Apgar test. Apgar stands for Activity, Pulse, Grimace, Appearance and Respiration, and she was perfect in every way. Like almost all father's, I melted the first time I cradled my child in my arms.

We took home *Baby Berkovich* from the hospital without a name. Barbara and I felt we needed to get to know our daughter before we could name her. We tried Ann, Anna, Hannah, and Zelda, and finally settled on Sarah. We called Israel first and checked with my grandmother Alte, who was also sometimes called Sarah to make sure we were allowed to name our daughter Sarah.

Alte told us her first name was not Sarah, but originally was Soshi, and now went by the name Alte Sarah Bat Leah. She only used Sarah when people didn't understand her Czech name Soshi, a name she had not used since an illness earlier in her life. Sarah's middle name, Rachael, was the name of my grandfather Meir's mother, or Sarah's great-great-grandmother's name. Barbara, thinking *Rachel* was spelled like *Michael,* ended up spelling Sarah's middle name as *Rachael* on all of her birth certificates and legal documents. Our daughter is now stuck with a misspelled middle name for the rest of her life.

When Sarah got home she would not stop wailing. We were new parents and didn't know if it was indigestion? Wanting to be nursed? Does she have gas? Does she need to be burped or changed? We tried everything. She just would not stop crying. We called the pediatrician and he told us this sounded like colic. Colic is defined as the unexplained crying for three or more hours at a time, at least three times a week, in an otherwise healthy baby. I have to admit I was not prepared for the crying. After a few days of sleep deprivation, Barbara looked like a bleary-eyed zombie. We tried a cornucopia of colic cures, tea, pacifiers, messages and back rubs, placing her atop of the vibrating washing machine, driving her past midnight in the car around the neighborhood, swaddling her in a blanket, singing to her, rocking her, swaying with her, pleading with her to stop her screaming, but nothing worked. I was sure as new parents we were doing something wrong. We were desperate and finally tried Mylicon drops, for babies with gas. Thankfully it seemed to work. We went through hell for three months because our child needed to fart.

Only ten months after Sarah's birth Barbara called me to let me know she was pregnant again. But this pregnancy was different from the first one. Barbara wasn't feeling well in the first few months and she went into premature labor at about her twenty-fourth week of pregnancy. Any baby born before the thirty-seventh week of pregnancy is considered preterm. These babies are at a significant risk for health problems relating to the brain, lungs, digestive system or even death.

Doctors aren't quite sure what all the causes of premature labor are, but stress seems to play a major role. Barbara was working up until she went into labor. I had recently lost my job as Chief Financial Officer of Malibu Valley Inc. I had worked for Charles Boudreau and his son Brian, who was my college roommate along with Kevin Hyman when we were living on Santa Monica Beach. Charles had passed away from cancer, and Brian needed to cut back on his expenses. My parent's marriage was beginning to unravel, and they were fighting all of the time, and we had a one-year-old baby who had worn us down with her colic. I think it is safe to say we were stressed at this time of our lives.

Barbara's preterm labor was stopped with a combination of full time bed rest and medications. She was on a Terbutaline pump, which administered a drug that was given intravenously to stop contractions. She also had to monitor her contractions and send the data over the phone to the doctor several times a day. We were really living on pins and needles during these few months. Since Barbara was on bed rest, we needed help with child care, meal preparations, and household tasks, so we hired a nanny, who also helped with the housekeeping. I spent my time looking for a new job and within two weeks found a consulting engagement with a time share company which covered my expenses for the short term.

Just past the thirty sixth week of Barb's pregnancy we went to AMI Tarzana Medical Center and had Dr. Rubenstein as our obstetrician again. We were in the same homey room where Sarah was born. It was January 22, 1991, and as we were watching TV in the delivery room Operation Desert Storm, the U.S. war to drive Iraqi forces from Kuwait, was unfolding. The dictator, Saddam Hussein, launched Scud missiles on Israel in an unsuccessful attempt to draw Israel into the war. Israel's largest cities Tel Aviv and Haifa were hit, but, miraculously, nobody was killed. Residents in Israel, including my grandparents, aunts, uncles and cousins, scrambled for the protective clothing and the masks that they had been given by the government because of fears that chemical weapons would be used. The whole experience seemed otherworldly. We felt like we were in a TV episode from the Twilight Zone.

Then all of a sudden the nurse who was monitoring our baby's heartbeat had a concerned look on her face. She immediately paged Dr. Rubenstein to come STAT, but there was no answer. I kept asking what was wrong, but she just ignored me. They began wheeling Barbara into the next room, which was used for emergency C-sections. After several more pages, Dr. Rubenstein finally entered the sterile operating room and took over. He said it was too late for the C-Section. The baby was about to be born. As its head came out, my heart sank. The baby didn't look quite right. The umbilical cord was wrapped tightly around its neck. Dr. Rubenstein quickly unwounded the cord and then after a few painful seconds we finally heard our baby cry.

It was a boy. He was a bluish-purple-colored boy. After Dr. Rubenstein suctioned his mouth and nose in an attempt to remove any fluids he swallowed in utero, the nurse gave him his Apgar test within the first minute of his life. He received a seven due to his color. The doctor then gave him a second test at about five minutes and he received an eight. Dr. Rubenstein turned to me and said, "He'll be fine. He weighed seven pounds ten ounces and was relatively healthy. "He will probably need to be kept in the hospital a few days," the doctor said. "He will need to be treated with ultraviolet lights, called billirubin lights, for jaundice." The lights looked like the ones used in fast food places to keep the French fries warm. After delivering our baby, we had to leave the hospital without him.

He only spent a few days in the neonatal unit, but it was still sad to drive home without our newborn.

Our son was named Aaron Benjamin Berkovich. Aaron was the name of my mother's cousin from Israel. He had recently passed away and Barbara I wanted to honor his memory. The biblical Aaron was Moses' older brother. He was the first Kohen Gadol or High Priest, or as the Hawaiian's would say, the Big Kahuna. Aaron was Moses' spokesperson and Israel's greatest peacemaker. When he heard two people arguing, he would go to each of them and tell them how much the other regretted his actions, until the two people faced each other as friends.

As our children grew, Sarah's bedtime routine had evolved around her self-professed fear of the dark. She gathered, or more often, her mommy gathered, the following items into a little nest before she would go to sleep. She required several pillows, at least three receiving blankets, Brown Bear (a stuffed animal Lily gave Sarah when she was born), Puppy (another stuffed animal), and her balloon blanket. Heaven forbid one of these objects was missing or that any of her blankets be "crumpled up." After everything was put in its place, Barbara would need to sleep beside Sarah and Aaron. But Barb would usually be the first one to fall asleep. I would often have to go looking for her and remind her she had her own bed. Sarah also had a fear of loud noises for a while, and would cry when she heard a mixer or saw. After a while she outgrew this fear. "I'm not afraid of the noises anymore, because I got Big," she would say, "and when I grow up, I want to be a grown-up!"

Our daughter could climb anything, her crib, her brother's crib, the sofa, trees. We always wondered where she got the energy to do this. She never ate her meat, and seemed to subsist only on Cheerios. When she did eat something other than Cheerios, it was slices of cheddar cheese, but not just any slices, they had to be thin enough to see light through. Any thicker than one or two millimeters and she would not eat it. We tried to adapt foods to child-friendly shapes and sizes for Sarah, but she would not eat anything new, no matter what we tried.

Aaron, on the other hand was an omnivore's dream, he ate everything, and he always had a happy disposition. He started using two word combinations at seventeen months. His favorite was "video me," which meant he wanted to watch himself on TV. He would sing songs like "EE-EI-EE-EI-OOO" from Old McDonald, and "Round and Round," from the wheels on the bus, and he loved for his mother to rock him and sing "Rock-a-bye Baby."

My children were first generation twenty-first-century American Jews. They were born here and belonged here. As Americans, they would grow and assimilate to the American culture, but hopefully they would continue to feel connected to the culture of their ancestors.

51. Attempted

I hate the sound of an ambulance siren. The loud high pitched shrieking assaults my ears. It makes me feel like my head is going to split open, especially as its wailing scream comes closer and closer.

My parent's marriage was like the Titanic cruising toward the iceberg. My mother was crying for attention, help and understanding. She was slipping, drowning, and emotionally circling the drain. My father was tired of having curses rain down on him, tired of being called a louse, loser, fool, and failure, tired of her depressive mood swings, and tired of the constant drama. I arrived at my parent's apartment as the paramedics were loading my mother on a gurney onto the ambulance. She had apparently ingested either a bottle of valium or sleeping pills. No one knew exactly how many she had taken. Both of these drugs were widely prescribed and available. Both were depressant drugs that slowed down the central nervous system. Suicidal people think if they take an overdose of sleeping pills they will just go to sleep and never wake up. What often happens instead is they wake up choking on their own vomit and due to a lack of oxygen incur brain damage.

As the ambulance speed up the street to Tarzana Regional Medical Center, I followed closely in my car. Tarzana was the same hospital my children were born in, and we were headed to the only other place I dreaded more than the delivery room, the emergency room.

Suicide is a complete betrayal of family and friends; it is a complete default of all responsibility. It leaves all those who care about the person bewildered and confused for the rest of their lives. In Judaism, the determination of life and death is not given to man, only G-d may grant or take a life, and only an egocentric person would commit suicide. Anyone who takes his own life is a murderer. Jewish cemeteries reserve a special section for suicides. People who commit this act are buried at the border of the cemetery near an outlying fence. They must be buried at least six feet away from any surrounding grave. It is the ultimate scarlet letter of shame. It is alienation for eternity.

My mother's skin, which was usually an olive color, was a pale ashen gray. She was given ipecac, to make her vomit. Then the doctor's made her drink a gruel looking substance, which was activated charcoal, to soak up the poison in her intestines before coming out in diarrhea induced by the magnesium citrate they were also giving her. Finally they ran a tube about the size of a thumb, bit by bit down her throat, into her stomach and pumped down a saline solution which they then sucked back up through the tube. Usually the doctors either require the patient to take the ipecac or they pump the stomach; they don't do both. But I think they were angry at my mother and they wanted to punish her.

In California if you attempt suicide the state requires you to be held for three days of psychiatric care. Sometimes it can be followed by an application to a judge who can require you to be held for up to a fourteen day period. Beyond that, a judge can have you committed or you can voluntarily enter a mental hospital. The psychiatrist who interviewed my mother was convinced she would not attempt to kill herself again. The tortuous process of having her stomach pumped and the anguish she caused her children was enough of a punishment to dissuade her from attempting it again, at least for the time being, and she was released within three days. There are people who threaten suicide and get ignored. My mother threatened suicide almost daily. She cried wolf so many times it was hard to take her seriously. She used her threats of killing herself like the Sword of Damocles over our heads. My sisters and I never knew when it would fall.

52. Severed Branches

I always thought my family was like an old oak tree with deep roots and branches extending from the trunk which would continue grow with each new generation. I have since discovered the bond holding my family together is not a super strong epoxy, but cheap Elmer's glue.

When people know each other well, it's very easy to say and do things that will hurt or anger the other person. My parents were experts at mutual button pushing. Their marriage was now dead, it was time for them to bury it, and get on with their lives. My sisters and I would now come from a broken home, and not only was our family broken, but something inside each of us was broken as well. Our disintegration meant holidays, birthdays and every special occasion in our lives would never be the same.

A divorce always affects children, even adult children, and our fractured family would split the loyalties of my sisters. We were wounded, angry, frustrated and had our own fears of abandonment and insecurities to deal with. Divorcing parents try to get you to side with one against the other. This is done either blatantly, by blaming the other parent, or subtly, by one parent being more needy and vulnerable than the other parent. While divorce may have liberated our father, it incarcerated us, and especially Vered, who was always closest to our mother. We all tried to support our mother; she was clearly the more fragile parent, but our mother demanded we not speak with our father, and it put us in a very precarious position.

Mom had been abandoned by her parents and was raised by her Bobbeh, and now she perceived the divorce as a second abandonment. She did not work during much of the marriage and was nervous and pressured about finances, and she wanted to fight for as much as she could get from my father and used us to achieve that end. The husband in most marriages usually has the money, so he threatens to cut it off. My father would often tell my mother "you will die poor and alone," the two things she feared the most in life. The wife typically has the kids, and she uses the loyalty of her children as a weapon against her husband. Divorce wars are just like nuclear wars; nobody ever wins.

My sisters hurt my father by what they said and did, and my father has since refused to talk to them. He says talking to them makes him physically sick and he no longer has the strength to try. I tried to intervene, only to be told to stay out of it. But as I see his skin sag and his heart weaken, all I think about is how sad the situation is. People in my family seem to want to wallow in self-pity. Maybe it's a family trait. Jamila didn't talk with her daughter, Sima. My father does not talk with Vered or Lily. Lily does not talk with her daughter, Eve. When we grew up, learning to hold a grudge seemed to be the rule. Maybe it's something we learned through the generations. We all have big disappointments and rejections in life, especially from people we are close to. Learning to let go and forgive never comes easily, but I know from my own experience, not having to carry around heavy grudges has made me feel better.

We chant a verse in synagogue on the Shabbath before Passover from the book of Malachi. "Before I send you Elijah the prophet, before the coming of the great and terrible day of the Lord, He shall turn the heart of fathers to the children, and the heart of the children to their fathers." (Malachi 3:23-24). Malachi spoke of the coming of the Messiah, and only after the Messiah comes will the hearts of parents turn to children and vice versa. Only then will parents and children get along. I only hope the members of my family don't wait until a Messiah shows up before they come to their senses and stop holding grudges.

53. Colorado

The beauty of Colorado, the natural landscape, the open views, and the majestic mountains comforted me in the knowledge that something out there was greater than my family problems or me. There was a magic there, a sense of possibility I didn't feel anywhere else.

Oved Anter, an Israeli friend we'd known since Brooklyn, was in the insulated and bizarre diamond trade, where millions of dollars of merchandise crisscrossed the globe on the strength of a handshake. Oved contacted me and requested I look into an investment he had made in Denver, Colorado. He had spent only a few minutes walking through an old building and bought it on the spot. He was used to making deals for millions of dollars on just a shake of the hand. Often deals were done with no checks, little documentation, and just based on his word. Since the Middle Ages the diamond trade had been dominated by Jews, and deals were always sealed with a handshake and the Yiddish phase, Mazel and Bracha, meaning luck and blessings. The diamond trade was made up a small group of people who operated in a circle of trust, and since I had known Oved from the time I was a child, I was a member of that circle.

Anter purchased the Symes Building constructed in 1906 with two other partners, Naty Saidoff, who was also a diamond dealer, and Oded Adler. The partnership they formed was called ASA associates. The historic building they bought consisted of ninety thousand square feet of office on the upper floors and retail space on the first floor and basement. It was nestled in the heart of Downtown

Denver on Champa Street and the 16th Street Mall. The Mall was a one-mile stretch of open-air pedestrian streets which were traversed by free shuttle buses carrying thousands of passengers up and down them daily. It was a place for aspiring musicians to play their instruments, downtown office workers to shop, work and grab a bite to eat; a place where gawkers and tourists could stroll, and where panhandlers mixed with the likes of Robot Man, a guy who wore a giant Afro wig and aluminum-colored tights and made sounds like a hydraulic machine as people walked by. Downtowns across the country were seeing a rebirth, and Denver's reinvigorated core was a prime example of what was possible.

The Symes building had all kinds of problems. It had extensive deferred maintenance issues and asbestos, and was last renovated when Jimmy Hendrix played Woodstock in the early 1960's. The floors were covered in green and orange shag carpeting; dark wood paneling lined the hallways, the public restrooms were antiquated, and it had no central air-conditioning system. The building had ancient electrical systems, elevators, and steam pipes. Everything was so old parts were no longer available for repairs. But in its own way the building was beautiful. It was designed by the New York firm of Hunt & Hunt in the Chicago School of architecture at the turn of the century. It was one of the first steel-framed buildings in Denver.

I knew the building needed work, but it had good bones. The lobby had black and gray marble flooring, detailed plaster ceilings, and etched brass elevator doors. Even though they had invested in the building, Naty and Oded, thought the property was a dog and wanted to sell it, but Oved didn't.

The building was anchored by the F.W. Woolworth Company. It was one of the original American five-and-dime stores which sold general merchandise. The Denver store at 174,000 square feet was the largest Woolworth variety store in the world. The Symes building had three floors leased to Woolworth, and the Woolworth's pension fund owned an adjacent building, which was attached to the first three floors of the Symes Building. The front door and entry to the store was through the Symes building on the 16th Street Mall. I was told the Woolworth lease had expired, and although Woolworth was still operating its business at this location, it was not responding to the lease renewal requests of the three Israeli owners.

Oved then made me an offer I could not refuse. He would lend me the money to buy a 15% stake in Symes, but the loan would carry a hefty 12% interest rate. Oved and I would be the only owners of the property and I would manage it. Even though I had zero experience managing properties, especially one with as many complicated issues as this one had, I agreed to the deal. But my agreement was subject to one condition. I would need to negotiate a new lease with F.W. Woolworth Company and I would only be required to invest in the project if Woolworth signed the lease I negotiated.

I couldn't believe my luck. I had absolutely nothing to lose. The market in Denver was severely depressed in the early 1990's and this asset was being purchased at substantially below replacement cost. The building was primarily vacant at the time, but it was located in the core of Downtown on 16th Street. If I could get Woolworth to sign a new lease, I could justify the purchase. Since I had no money, Oved's loaning me hundreds of thousands of dollars meant if things went well I had a substantial upside and, if things didn't, I would lose my share in the building, a share I wouldn't have had anyhow.

Bill Judy, the Woolworth Director of Real Estate in New York, was an old-time tough New York real estate professional, and he was the man I had to negotiate with. He told me "Kid, I've been around the block a few times, and I'm not certain we want to renew this lease." I responded politely, "Mr. Judy, I'm new to the real estate business, and I may be a simple country accountant from Colorado, but I can tell you, if the lease we are proposing isn't signed in the next two weeks, Woolworth will have to vacate the premises and pay us our hold-over rate from the time our lease expires. In addition, the 110,000 square foot building owned by your pension fund won't be worth a dime, especially if we restore the wall that used to exist between our two buildings."

Two weeks later, I had an executed ten-year lease with a rent increase of three hundred percent over the previous lease from F.W. Woolworth. Mr. Judy, shortly after concluding this deal with me, mysteriously retired from the company. Had he refused my outrageous rent increase, I could have just walked away from the deal. He just couldn't understand why I was so nonchalant about whether they renewed their lease or not.

My family moved to Colorado at the end of December, 1992. When we arrived in Denver, we were greeted by a powerful winter storm with rain, snow, and freezing winds. The plummeting temperatures were well below freezing. As we disembarked the plane from California we realized how unprepared we were. We didn't own any boots, heavy jackets or gloves. Also, not knowing how to drive on ice, I skidded several times on the treacherous roads as we left the airport.

Sarah, who was three years old at the time, had an ear infection. She was crying the entire flight. The flight reminded me of what it must have been like for my parents on their initial voyage to New York with me as a baby with an ear infection on the ship. When we arrived in Denver, the first thing we did was look up a pediatrician in the phone book and headed to his office.

I rented a house in a nice neighborhood called Gun Club Green. Thankfully, the place had nothing to do with guns. Our furniture was supposed to arrive any day, so we slept on the floor in sleeping bags. North American Van Lines was the only company which guaranteed delivery over New Year, so we hired them. After they loaded all of our possessions on the truck, we discovered they lied to us, and were going to unload our household items in a storage facility in California. We were about to go to the airport and there wasn't time for us to do anything about the situation. North American said we would have to wait until they could find a driver heading east to Denver. Each morning they would tell us our furniture was on its way, only to be told the next day, it was still in the warehouse. We slept on the floor for two weeks thinking that day would be the last day and our stuff would arrive shortly. When the movers finally showed up, the driver demanded a cashier's check before he would begin to unload. As the boxes were brought into the house we noticed many were crushed. The driver said half jokingly, "Go ahead … file a claim." The final insult occurred as the North American Van left and we watched as the driver backed the huge truck into our Toyota Camry and smashed its front end.

We eventually did get settled in our home, and working downtown was initially exciting. Everything was new, and the job was challenging, although I quickly learned that no one loves a landlord. I never received a thank you, a hug, or a wish of success. Landlords never receive any form of appreciation. Our building was one hundred years old, but my tenants couldn't understand why things would break down. They had no patience or sympathy for me when things went wrong.

Getting stuck in our elevators was a big issue. Tenants would hyperventilate and then scream at me when they dropped one or two floors before the elevator came to a stop.

"We test the breaks annually. They have never failed yet," I would say with confidence. But my tenants could care less. They were very impatient for the half-hour or hour if often it took the Elevator Company or Denver Fire Department to extract them.

Then there were those tenants who would come into my office dripping wet and actually demand I pay for their dry cleaning.

"Why should I pay for your dry cleaning?" I said.

"Because," they would respond exasperated, "Your toilets flush UP. All I did was hit the flush valve handle and the water shot UP all over me."

"From time to time we have water pressure problems. When the water level runs low on the upper floors, the pump kicks on. Sometimes it kicks on at very inopportune times," I would respond.

At least once a month, fire alarms would just go off. We never had a real fire, thank goodness. The smoke detectors on top of the elevator shafts were very sensitive and as the elevators went up and down they would create a vacuum and kick up dust in the shaft. The dust would then set off the smoke alarms. Denver's Fire Department would not allow me to change the smoke detectors to heat detectors, so it meant we would have the fire alarms go off at least once a month. This would be our monthly reminder to dust the top of the elevator cabs. It was a good thing we never had a fire. After a while, our tenants were conditioned to ignore the alarms.

Winter in the Symes building was hammer season. Tenants would come into my office and say, "Someone is banging on our pipes with what sounds like a baseball bat. We can't work with that kind of noise."

"Nah," I would respond bluntly, "It's our steam heating system. When water condenses in the radiators and then gets hit with hot steam, our pipes bang a little. It will stop as soon as the water in the radiator turns back into steam."

"Well the banging just knocked my coat rack off the wall, and the knocking is so violent and loud, it sounds like it's about to burst and kill someone," they would say.

"Don't worry, I'm insured if that happens." I said.

I never understood why, but each time I tried to raise the rents in the building tenants would really give me a hard time.

After managing the Symes building for a few years I was ready for the next deal. Another building up the street from Symes was coming on the market. The owner, Brookfield Properties, purchased it along with a portfolio of A class properties and wanted to sell this C class property by year end. It was the end of November already and it meant we needed to move fast. I took the deal to Oved, but he didn't have that kind of cash available at the time and could not perform. So I called Naty Saidoff, Oved's former partner, and asked him if he would be interested. Naty was impressed with what I had done with the Symes building, and he wanted to do business with me. We purchased the 189,000 square foot 1957 vintage Petroleum Building in cash with a ten day due diligence period and a closing within thirty days of our contract. It was a great building on the 16th Street Mall and had wonderful views of Denver's capital. The only reason it hadn't leased prior to our acquisition was that the brokers at Brookfield didn't like C-class properties; their other properties were all A-class and prestigious. Leasing this kind of property wasn't worth their time. Within nine months of our acquisition we were one hundred per cent occupied. We were also now one of the City and County of Denver's largest landlords.

After 117 years, Woolworth announced it was getting out of the general merchandising business, closing four hundred stores, and laying off over nine thousand employees. Our store in Denver was one of the four hundred stores to be closed. Bill Judy wasn't kidding me when he said he wasn't sure if they wanted to renew their lease. What at the time appeared to be one of the worst things to happen turned out to be the best. Woolworth continued paying their rent. Their pension fund agreed to sell us the vacant, ugly, 110,000-square-foot large box of a building with no windows. Through sheer luck of being in the right place at the right time, we were in the midst of a data explosion due to growth in a relatively new technology called the internet.

The internet gave rise to unprecedented demand by telecom companies for large blocks of space. The space they needed had to be concentrated in a central business district. It had to be near a high-tech fiber optic corridor and had to have extra heavy floor loads to handle the racks and racks of equipment. They needed high ceilings for the air-conditioning and cabling for the servers and telecommunication equipment. Land in the central business district was in limited supply, and we met all of the criteria these data centers, known as telecom hotels, required.

Norm Waite Jr., the billionaire who started Gateway Computers with his brother Ted, decided to invest in telecom hotels. Norm, through his representative, Jim Duggan, contacted me a few months after we purchased the 110,000-square-foot building from Woolworth. He wanted to acquire the building we had purchased just a few months earlier. We agreed to sell it to him for nine times our purchase price. I always said I'd rather be lucky than smart. Although the Symes and Petroleum buildings had appreciated substantially over the years, those values were on paper. Norm Waite's money was in our bank, and it was real. For the first few days after the transaction was completed, I would call our bank's customer service number several times a day, just to confirm the funds were still there. I liked listening to the digitized voice say the word "million" over and over.

54. The Blunder Years

They say the pain men experience puts hair on their chests as it removes it from their heads. Maybe that's why I'm bald and my chest looks like a bear skin rug.

As the years passed in Colorado our children entered the thick fog of adolescence. It seemed to be a time we all lost our bearings. Our children's teen years were filled with amplified emotions. Windows in our home often rattled with the thunder of slamming doors. It seemed like just a short time ago they were kind, adorable, cooperative toddlers. All of a sudden we had willful, self-absorbed and reckless teens.

As our daughter Sarah approached her sixteenth birthday, she became impatient and moody. Like most people, she needed to learn how to be alone, without being lonely. Maybe risky, dangerous behavior is encoded in our genes. Maybe that's why teenagers drive too fast, drink too much, and just act like idiots. Even though Sarah had some very high voltage crackling through the wires of her brain, something must have short circuited. I always wondered whether nature or nurture makes the biggest difference in how children turn out. How exactly does the murky chromosomal matter mix with the nurturing our kids receive? How do we get them to avoid the same mistakes we made at their age, or keep them from discovering new ones we didn't make?

Our son, Aaron, at sixteen is very different from his sister. By the age of sixteen, he knows everything there is to know in the world. Young Mr. Berkovich has yet to discover clothes can actually be hung in a closet, or if they are dirty, placed in a laundry bin. I'm pretty sure he has carpeting in his room. I remember seeing it when we first moved into our house. It would be a miracle if he would only pick up all of the junk food wrappers and clothes off his floor. Aaron is also under the impression aerosol sprays have replaced showering. A little water dabbled on his head is equivalent to a shampoo. Our son has the uncanny ability to study for tests while he is playing video games and instant messaging his friends, all at the same time. He assures me these multitasking skills will come in handy later in life, but I am not convinced. Our son has also learned how to corner us when we are in a good mood and he has figured out which parent is most likely to cave in first. All of Aaron's acquisitions are for worthy causes. He knows spending money on frivolous things won't cut it, so he tells us everything is "educational." I could try giving my son all kinds of advice, but he already knows everything, and doesn't have any room in his brain for my gibberish. But I'm certain this is just a phase of adolescence, and this too will surely pass.

Midlife crisis has long been thought of as something only men go through, as a period of adult adolescent regression. But these days, women have come to experience their own version of these upheavals, and it's more than just wrestling with their hormones through this stage of life. The causes and reactions to these midlife transitions appear to be very different for men and women. Male midlife issues usually revolve around work and career. It's about how men measure up on the economic and social ladder. So they usually run out and buy red sports cars and get themselves new trophy wives at forty. Women are more likely than men to have their crisis begin with a family problem, and their turmoil is more likely to be driven by introspection, and a reassessment of values and goals. Barbara went through her midlife crisis as our children were blundering through their adolescence. She decided to take Aaron and move to

San Diego, while I stayed in Colorado with Sarah as she finished her senior year of high school. She needed to step out from under my shadow, and dreamt of starting her own business. She wanted to control her own destiny and realize her own dreams.

I had achieved financial success. I had over one hundred employees and an impressive balance sheet. By all accounts I should have been happy, but I was miserable. It seemed my phone constantly rang with one problem after another. Although all of the various businesses I was in were successful, the combined energy and oversight required took a substantial emotional and physical toll.

Taking control is something I do unconsciously almost reflexively. The same traits which made me successful in business harmed me at home. I was used to telling people what to do and having them follow my orders. But the same rules of business do not apply at home. It's very difficult to switch from a work mode to a home mode. In many ways, I know I was unkind by inattention to my family. I was constantly wrapped up with work-related problems. I came home exhausted, angry, and short tempered. I had an unrelenting pain in my back and down one of my legs, and was not sleeping well. I took so many over-the-counter anti-inflammatory pain killers I required surgery just to fix the damage I had caused my intestines. I was also beginning to begrudge my family the freedom they had, and the fact I worked all of the time and they seemed not to notice or appreciate it. The most important thing I lost during this time was the ability to enjoy the small moments in life.

The author, Harvey Mackay, once wrote about a man who gave a eulogy at a friend's funeral. He spoke of the dates on the tombstone, and noted that first came the date of birth and then the date the friend passed away. At the eulogy the man said what mattered most of all was the dash between those years. For that dash represented the time his friend spent alive on this earth. For it matters not how much we own, the cars, the house and the cash. What matters is how we live and love, and how we spend our dash.

55. Finding Home

I put my finger on Israel on the large globe in my office and then lift it ever so slightly as I spin the earth one and a half revolutions, and as it stops my finger points to San Diego, California. This city sits exactly on the same thirty two degree north latitudinal parallel as Israel. It is a straight shot half way across the earth. Like Israel, San Diego has deep canyons separating its mesas with lots of natural parkland scattered throughout the city, and it also has many dense urban communities. The climate is semi-arid, sunny and mild, a lot like the Mediterranean climate. We now live in a place where the seam of the horizon to the west is visible just as the sun sets over the Pacific Ocean and where bright-colored hot air balloons float over our house. We are often walloped by San Diego's beauty, and it's the place we now call home.

But San Diego is not Jerusalem, Tel Aviv, or Petach Tikvah. It seems like all Jewish odysseys start with a dispersion or exile and conclude with a return or homecoming. My family's story is no different. Even though Jews wandered the globe for over two thousand years and although we were still able to guard our oldest traditions and rituals and preserve our Jewish identity, it seems that no matter where we went we were still just aliens in a foreign land, everywhere, that is, but Israel.

My family traveled very far in their lives only to wind up steps away from where they began. They trekked half way around the planet trying to find a place on this earth they could call their own, a place where they belonged and fit in. But they always longed to return to their roots, where the soil and sun nourished their souls, and where they felt whole. For some these roots go so deep they just can't be pulled out. My family needs to live in a place where the natural landscape, the spoken language, the customs, friends and family make them feel—this is home.

When her Bobbeh died, Emmah inherited a third of the land with its shack and the orange grove where she grew up in Herzliya. The other two thirds were given to her father's two sons, who were her half brothers. Emmah purchased the land from her two half brothers and in a deal with a local developer received the penthouse of the apartment building that was constructed on it. My mother literally lives on the ground where she picked a flower as a little girl on that Sabbath day and thought G-d would soon strike her down. Since being hit by lightning is still one of her concerns, we made certain her building has a grounded lightning rod on the roof, so she appears to be safe for now.

Abbah lives in Petach Tikvah, around the corner from Broide Street, where my grandparents', Meir and Alte's, house once stood. Petach Tikvah was the first modern Jewish agricultural settlement in Israel; that is why Meir chose it. The extensive citrus groves which ringed the city have since disappeared as real estate developers acquired land for construction projects. My father and his sisters inherited the land they grew up on and constructed apartments on it, which they rent out. Abbah now lives only a few blocks away from his sisters Zipora and Esther.

My sister Lily lives in Jerusalem, the holiest city in Judaism and the spiritual center of the Jewish people. It is the capital of Israel and its largest city in terms of both population and area. Ironically, Jerusalem means a legacy or inheritance of peace. Unfortunately, this city has never had much peace, but the hope is that one day the legacy will be realized. Jerusalem is situated on a plateau in the Judean mountains and all of the homes, apartments, and other buildings are built of the same Jerusalem stone, a golden limestone that glows as it absorbs the sun's rays. Lily is raising her own tribe of Israel in a home that has an awesome view of the valley and the Old City.

Will Rogers once referred to Los Angeles as a place where too many people spend money they haven't earned to buy things they don't want to impress people they don't like. Vered and Pini were living in Los Angeles and wanted to simplify their life. They were tired of racing to buy clothes, shoes, televisions, and just stuff. They were searching for a more minimalistic existence, where less would be more. If they stayed in Los Angeles, they knew David and Danielle would go on to college in the United States and since they wanted to remain close to their children, they would never be able to move back to Israel if they waited until their children graduated. English became the only language spoken at home. When Pini started saying things like "I beg your pardon, excuse me, I don't understand your meaning," Vered knew it would be too late to make a change if they didn't do it soon. So Vered and Pini, along with Danielle and David, moved to Tel Aviv, the most modern and metropolitan area of Israel.

But the problem with simple living is that even though it can be rewarding and joyful, it is never simple. Israel is a complicated place. The key to survival there is having a keen sense of humor and lots of *savlanut,* the Hebrew word for patience. Driving a car, shopping, seeing a doctor, and everyday experiences we take for granted in the United States are difficult. The roads are narrow. Cars double-park everywhere. An open parking space can cause a stampede of Israelis or an all out war. The sounds of horns honking and people yelling at each are normal. But the same drivers who cuss at you and flip you birds will immediately pull over and offer you help if it looks like you need it. Security is a concern. Having to open your hand bag before you enter a grocery store or being felt up by a guard when going to a movie theatre is something you learn to live with. Here, if you invite someone out for a drink, it means coffee, not cocktails. Israelis who want to go up in an elevator will push the down button because they are certain it makes the elevator come down to get them. If they are polite they ask you if they can help themselves to your fridge, otherwise they don't even ask. When there's a bank line, it's not atypical for some women who just walked through the front door to go straight to the front of the teller line and say "*Ani hayitti po kodem,*" which means I was here before, and then she cuts in line and acts like her place was saved. At the post office it's not unheard of to discover they have run out of stamps. If you ask them, "Why are you open if you don't have stamps?" they will look at you like you are stupid and say, "What do you mean, of course we are open. We're the post office." Neighbors have been known to call you up and say, "We wanted to make sure you are home. Your window is open, but we can't see you. Could you move over to the right, so we can see you?" Yet even though Israelis have been known to make life difficult for one another, they also care for one another. If anything, sometimes they care too much.

I am a dual national, American and Israeli, but being American doesn't make me less an Israeli. I am proud to be both. Israel gave birth to me, and the United States educated and nurtured me. I may be the only one in my family who has been able to straddle the American-Israeli cultural divide. Although I have lived in this new world for most of my life I feel equally as comfortable in the old world.

Legal Aliens: it isn't that America considers my family alien. America accepted us. It's that my family considers the environment here to be alien to them. Most of us need to be in a place where we sense we are in our natural world, and for my family that place is Israel.

Epilogue

I tried to write down the stories I remembered before they faded away. I obviously don't have an encyclopedic mind or a flawless memory and apologize if other members of the family remember things differently.

Like most people's lives, ours are not divided into absolutes. No one in our family was meant to be depicted as entirely a villain or a hero, good or bad, black or white. We are far more complicated than that.

I hope you all enjoy the read.

978-0-595-51484-7
0-595-51484-7